All You Need is a Wink and

The Naughty Secretary Club *is packed with more than 50 fun, secretary-themed jewelry projects including necklaces, bracelets, earrings and more! Learn how to transform almost anything (and we mean ANYTHING) into a fun charm, use shredded junk mail in a craftalicious piece of art or alter paperclips to make a fabulous necklace. Break out of the mundane and tap into your inner "Naughty Secretary" today.*

#Z2123 • NORTH LIGHT BOOKS

by Jennifer Perkins

Jennifer is the host of two popular television craft shows, a member of the Austin Craft Mafia and her jewelry has been featured in various magazines including Seventeen, Marie Claire and Bust.

You can find this book and many other North Light books at your favorite bookseller (including BarnesandNoble.com, Borders.com, Amazon.com and BookSense.com). Or order by calling 1-800-258-0929, or visit us online at www.mycraftivityshop.com.

NORTH LIGHT BOOKS
an imprint of
F+W Publications, Inc.

JOIN A WORLD OF CRAFTERS AT **WWW.MYCRAFTIVITY.COM** CONNECT. CREATE. EXPLORE.

Volume 08

Craft:
transforming traditional crafts

Special Section

FREE POCKET LOOM page 48

Features

Columns

Vol. 08, August 2008. CRAFT (ISSN 1932-9121) is published 4 times a year by O'Reilly Media, Inc. in the months of January, April, July, and October. O'Reilly Media is located at 1005 Gravenstein Hwy. North, Sebastopol, CA 95472, (707) 827-7000. SUBSCRIPTIONS: Send all subscription requests to CRAFT, P.O. Box 17046, North Hollywood, CA 91615-9588 or subscribe online at craftzine.com/subscribe or via phone at (866) 368-5652 (U.S. and Canada), all other countries call (818) 487-2037. Subscriptions are available for $34.95 for 1 year (4 issues) in the United States; in Canada: $39.95 USD; all other countries: $49.95 USD. Application to Mail at Periodicals Postage Rates is Pending at Sebastopol, CA, and at additional mailing offices. POSTMASTER: Send address changes to CRAFT, P.O. Box 17046, North Hollywood, CA 91615-9588. Canada Post Publications Mail Agreement Number 41129568. Canada Postmaster: Send address changes to: O'Reilly Media, PO Box 456, Niagara Falls, ON L2E 6V2.

Maker SHED
DIY KITS + TOOLS + BOOKS + FUN

makershed.com

SOCK MONKEY
This creative starter kit will have you making a "Finnoola Peach" monkey faster than you can say "eek eek."

SUBLIME STITCHING
One tidy package with everything you need to get started stitching, even if you've never held a needle and thread.

FASHIONING TECHNOLOGY
Get the top book on smart crafting, because LEDs are the new sequins.

SUSHI WALLET
A great starter felting project. You'll be addicted to knitting these little morsels. Kit includes three "a la carte" pattern options.

MONSTER KITS
Make a friendly neighborhood mini-monster, as seen in CRAFT, Volume 06. No two mini-monster kits are alike. Good for all skill levels.

LED HULA HOOPS
As shown in CRAFT, Volume 06, with the right parts you can make your very own LED Hula Hoop. Because sometimes you want to dance in the dark.

Craft:® Projects

Craft: Volume 08

Crafter Profiles

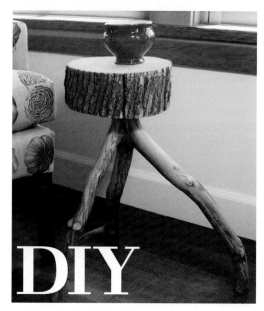

DIY

Make Cool Stuff

28

ON THE COVER
Travis Meinolf wants to teach us how to weave. Behold his portable cardstock loom, free in this issue, and instructions on how to learn this age-old craft on page 48. Photograph by Cody Pickens. Illustration by Nick Dragotta.

105

Craft:
transforming traditional crafts

EDITOR AND PUBLISHER
Dale Dougherty
dale@oreilly.com

EDITOR-IN-CHIEF
Tina Barseghian
tina@craftzine.com

CREATIVE DIRECTOR
Daniel Carter
dcarter@oreilly.com

MANAGING EDITOR
Shawn Connally
shawn@craftzine.com

DESIGNERS
Katie Wilson
Alison Kendall

ASSOCIATE MANAGING EDITOR
Goli Mohammadi
goli@craftzine.com

PRODUCTION DESIGNER
Gerry Arrington

PROJECTS EDITOR
Carla Sinclair

PHOTO EDITOR
Sam Murphy
smurphy@oreilly.com

SENIOR EDITOR
Natalie Zee Drieu
nat@craftzine.com

ASSOCIATE PUBLISHER
Dan Woods
dan@oreilly.com

COPY CHIEF
Keith Hammond

CIRCULATION DIRECTOR
Heather Harmon

ONLINE MANAGER
Tatia Wieland-Garcia

ACCOUNT MANAGER
Katie Dougherty
katie@oreilly.com

STAFF EDITOR
Arwen O'Reilly Griffith

CONTRIBUTING EDITOR
Phillip Torrone

MARKETING & EVENTS MANAGER
Rob Bullington

CRAFT TECHNICAL ADVISORY BOARD
**Jill Bliss, Jenny Hart, Garth Johnson,
Leah Kramer, Alison Lewis, Matt Maranian,
Ulla-Maaria Engeström, Kathreen Ricketson**

PUBLISHED BY O'REILLY MEDIA, INC.
Tim O'Reilly, CEO
Laura Baldwin, COO

Visit us online at craftzine.com
Comments may be sent to **editor@craftzine.com**

For advertising inquiries, contact:
Katie Dougherty, 707-827-7272, katie@oreilly.com

For Maker Faire and other event inquiries, contact:
Sherry Huss, 707-827-7074, sherry@oreilly.com

NOW GREENER THAN EVER!
CRAFT is now printed on recycled, acid-free paper with 30% post-consumer waste. Subscriber copies of CRAFT, Volume 08, were shipped in recyclable plastic bags.

PLEASE NOTE: Technology, the laws, and limitations imposed by manufacturers and content owners are constantly changing. Thus, some of the projects described may not work, may be inconsistent with current laws or user agreements, or may damage or adversely affect some equipment. Your safety is your own responsibility, including proper use of equipment and safety gear, and determining whether you have adequate skill and experience. Power tools, electricity, and other resources used for these projects are dangerous, unless used properly and with adequate precautions, including safety gear. Some illustrative photos do not depict safety precautions or equipment, in order to show the project steps more clearly. These projects are not intended for use by children.
Use of the instructions and suggestions in CRAFT is at your own risk. O'Reilly Media, Inc., disclaims all responsibility for any resulting damage, injury, or expense. It is your responsibility to make sure that your activities comply with applicable laws, including copyright.

Contributing Artists:
Natalia Chocron, Nick Dragotta, Dustin Fenstermacher, Saul Griffith, Samantha Hahn, Dustin Amery Hostetler, John Keatley, Tim Lillis, Garry McLeod, Virginia Meyers, Branca Nietzsche, Cody Pickens, Nik Schulz, Jen Siska

Contributing Writers:
Grace Bonney, Susan M. Brackney, Susie Bright, Lindsay Brown, Annie Buckley, Cathy Callahan, Jodie Carleton, Krystina Castella, Sally Converse-Doucette, Phil Daniel, Anna Dilemna, Ulla-Maaria Engeström, Victoria Everman, Sarah Gee, Diane Gilleland, Liz Gipson, Molly Graber, Saul Griffith, Christine Haynes, Joan Sheridan Hoover, Katie Kurtz, Shawnee Langworthy, Lisa Shobhana Mason, Nellie McKesson, Travis Meinolf, Chris Merrick, Syne Mitchell, Mark Montano, Brookelynn Morris, Becca Olsen, Abi Cotler O'Roarty, Jane Patrick, Kristen Roach, Peter Sheridan, Maggie Stewart, Joe Szuecs, Wendy Tremayne, Megan Mansell Williams

Bloggers: Michelle Kempner, Jenny Ryan, Becky Stern

Interns: Matthew Dalton (engr.), Adrienne Foreman (web), Kris Magri (engr.), Lindsey North (crafts), Meara O'Reilly (crafts), Ed Troxell (edit)

Customer Service cs@readerservices.craftzine.com
Manage your account online, including change of address at:
craftzine.com/account
866-368-5652 toll-free in U.S. and Canada
818-487-2037, 5 a.m.–5 p.m., Pacific

Grace Bonney (*DIY Design column*) is a foodie trapped in the body of a design addict. She lives in Brooklyn, N.Y., with her fiancé, and has been running her blog Design*Sponge since 2004. She's a hopeless reality TV fan, the doting mom of two finicky cats (Ms. Jackson and Turk), and a Southerner who's still trying to find the genteel side of her city of residence. Her newest project involves working with local artists and craftsmen to remodel the home of a Brooklyn family in need.

Cody Pickens (*Meinolf profile, Woven Vest project, Play, and cover*) is a San Francisco-based portrait photographer. When not on assignment, he enjoys riding his bike, playing tennis, and listening to any album on the Plastic City label. Recent inspirations include Julian Schnabel's cinematic masterpiece, the anticipation of whatever Ricky Gervais is working on, and Leipheimer going for yellow in the Tour de France. Cody resides in San Francisco with his girlfriend, Nancy, and their two feline companions. codypickens.com

Meara O'Reilly (*CRAFT intern*) has tested the fields of psychoacoustics, sound installation, pop music, and piano tuning, and has a growing interest in conductive textiles, heirloom technology, sustainable housing, and children's science education. When not on tour with a homemade gamelan instrument made out of forks and horsehair, she works at CRAFT making projects and keeping an eye on our crafted archive.

When he's not trying to figure out how looms work for CRAFT, or collecting and selling vintage posters (see his collection at jetsetposters.com), illustrator **Nik Schulz** (*Weaving Basics and Weaving Resources*) has a penchant for exploring and — truth be told — a fascination with Bigfoot. Over a recent dinner with friends, he outlined the case for the creature's existence; they all smiled and thought he was nuts. He also enjoys bocce ball, an interest that he finds raises fewer eyebrows.

Sarah Gee and **Lindsay Brown** (*Vintage Scarf Bedcover*) are designers living and working in Vancouver, B.C.'s Downtown Eastside, together forming Ouno Design. A schoolyard separates their studios, so they can just yell ideas across. Sarah and Lindsay prefer the textures of older materials, and they like modernist graphics by past masters such as Peter Perritt and Vera Neumann. They source vintage materials from anyplace they can: thrift stores, the rag warehouse, trunks in attics. Vanguards for the lounging lifestyle, they're excited about reintroducing floor pillows to the world.

Writer and artist **Annie Buckley** (*Art vs. Craft feature*) is lucky because her job is really fun: she spends most of her time looking at, making, or writing about art. Annie writes children's books, practices yoga, and recently finished a series of large photo collages of women turning into trees. She shares a home studio/office in Hollywood with her husband, Dane (his side is full of wires and circuits, hers has piles of papers and pictures), and their cats, Rex and Ricky.

Basically, **Mark Montano** (*Faux Stained Glass project*) is a craftaholic who likes to glue things together while hanging out in his underwear. He absolutely refuses to do anything unless it's fun; it's his number-one rule in life. Mark just started writing his next book, *Craftastic Home*, which is "like Willy Wonka works at Michaels craft store instead of at a chocolate factory." He lives in New York and works in Los Angeles. Recently fascinated with heat, he can be found melting whatever he gets his hands on.

Tina Barseghian
Welcome

≫ Tina Barseghian is editor-in-chief of CRAFT magazine.
tina@craftzine.com

The Name Game

The word *craft* has come under serious scrutiny lately. There's been debate between "trained" craftspeople and "untrained" crafters, between "contemporary art" and "craft," even between "design" and "craft." Craft itself has been even further qualified: traditional craft, indie craft, alternative craft, extreme craft. It's hard to believe we're all addressing the same subject.

A few months ago, I attended a talk by Jennifer Scanlan, associate curator of the Museum of Arts and Design in New York. With an entertaining slideshow, Scanlan showed examples of where art and craft intersect, then explained why the institution had recently changed its name from American Craft Museum to the Museum of Arts and Design: in short, because "people's association with the term *craft* did not reflect what was going on with our galleries."

"We felt that a more expansive name would allow us to address the shifting nature of the field itself," Scanlan said. "A lot of artists have been moving in between fields that had been more clearly defined 20 or 30 years ago. As a contemporary art museum, we wanted to show these artists, and to engage them."

Scanlan explained that a focus group had indicated that the word *craft* somehow implied the "vernacular and unsophisticated." On the other hand, "contemporary design these days is often associated with the idea of process, and using more traditional skills," she says. In other words, craft?

As a magazine dedicated to craft projects of all types, we present a range of crafts that dance along the blurry boundaries of art and craft, and bounce between indie, alt, extreme, and traditional crafts.

Making a modern stained glass window (*page 80*): traditional craft or art? A gorgeous end table made out of a tree trunk and branches (*page 101*): design or craft? A Polaroid photo transfer (*page 120*): contemporary art or craft? A sculpture built of bottle caps (*page 148*): sculptural art or craft?

We explore this tension explicitly in a feature article by Annie Buckley (*page 34*). Buckley confirms that museums and galleries are increasingly featuring works by contemporary artists who use traditional crafting techniques. And yet a pronounced bias from the art world against craft persists.

In the end, it's all semantics, as our cover subject Travis Meinolf would tell you. Meinolf shows that even the most traditional craft — weaving — defies category. He earned his master's degree in fine arts from the California College of the Arts (formerly the California College of Arts *and Crafts*, named after the burgeoning Arts and Crafts movement of the early 1900s) and chose to focus his thesis on weaving. Meinolf hand-wove dozens of woolen blankets as part of a conceptual art project, and gave them away for free (*page 46*). He's also designed a free, portable loom to prove that cloth can be made by anyone, anywhere. Does the fact that he teaches weaving and has his work exhibited at galleries and museums make weaving art instead of craft?

For us, craft is inherently about the creative process, whether practiced for years or in the hands of a beginner. Crafting may result in an artwork displayed in a vitrine in a museum, or a private treasure that never leaves the confines of your house. The important part of the equation here is not the category to which we assign it, but, as Scanlan says, the process by which it was made. Whether the person who created the object found joy in the discovery of a way to make something by hand, in learning about or mastering a technique.

We share with you these processes and discoveries, along with the stories of creators, in hopes of inspiring you to create — and not just based on patterns and ideas we provide. We encourage you to make your own design, and to share it with others. What you call it is up to you. ✕

the glitterer

self portrait no. 10

BLUE GLITTER MARKER
How I make my writing as dazzling as my artwork.

TOURMALINE GLITTER
What can often be found under my nails and on the end of my nose.

YOU
ARE
INVITED

THIS WEEKEND'S PARTY SHOES
Because anything that comes within 10 feet of my crafts table is fair game.

ROYAL BUTTERFLY CRAFT PUNCH
That makes shapes so pretty they almost don't need glitter. Almost.

CREATIVE. LIVING.

▶▶ Letters

My son and I walk together to school in Brooklyn each day, in all weather. On rainy days, I would normally cover his wheeled backpack with a plastic bag from the supermarket — not terribly efficient. The bags were usually too small, they'd slide off, they couldn't be used again, etc.

I was so pleased to see Diana Baker's "Recycle It" column featuring ways to reuse fabric from a broken umbrella as a weather cover for items like backpacks and laptops [*Volume 07, page 148,* "The Other Life of Umbrellas"]. I grabbed my recently broken umbrella from my office, bought a $1.50 length of stretch cord, and made a backpack cover this weekend. I'm thrilled with the finished results. Thank you.

—*Jennifer Wysokowski, Brooklyn, N.Y.*

I was so happy to see Annie Mohaupt and her Mohop shoes profiled [*Volume 07, page 42,* "Design-As-You-Wear Sandals"]. I bought a pair of her shoes through her website (mohop.com) last year and I love them. Not only are the shoes fantastic, but the customer service was impeccable. I have been speaking her praise since I got them, and I get compliments whenever I wear them. I am going to buy another pair ... if only I could decide which ones!

Thanks for the great article, and thanks to Annie for the DIY sandal instructions.

—*Aimee Santeler, Middletown, Conn.*

Could you please tell me, in the article "Simply Socks" by Meredith Davey [*Volume 07, page 120*]: what sock yarn did they use for that patterned green, blue, and gray sock on the opening page? Thank you.

—*Jessica Egmont, Gloucester, Mass.*

Editor's Note: Our staff editor Arwen O'Reilly Griffith knit those particular socks, and she used Opal Hundertwasser yarn, 75% Superwash virgin wool, 25% polyamide, in color 1432. We're certain you're not the only crafter wondering!

🔍 DARN IT!

Map Coffee Table author Mary Anderson's middle name isn't Jane, it's Elizabeth [*Volume 07, page 9*, "Contributors"]. We saw her business name, Marajane Creations, and jumped to conclusions. We apologize, Mary!

I love CRAFT magazine so much that I read and reread it cover-to-cover. When I read "Simply Socks" [*Volume 07, page 120*] I was surprised that the heel pattern was referred to as "Eye of Partridge." I'm sure you've gotten messages from several other rabid sock knitters advising you that the Eye of Partridge heel flap is a 4-row pattern:

EYE-OF-PARTRIDGE HEEL FLAP
NOTE: All slipped stitches are slipped purlwise.
Row 1: Slip the first stitch, K1, slip 1 across, ending with K1.
Row 2: Slip the first stitch, P across.
Row 3: Slip the first 2 stitches, K1, slip 1 across, ending with slip 1.
Row 4: P across.
Repeat these 4 rows until you have 2" or the distance from your anklebone to the floor. End after completing a purl row.

Your magazine does so much to inspire and inform, I thought you might appreciate support in providing correct information.

—*Jennifer A. Meyers, New Milford, Conn.*

Thanks for setting us straight, Jennifer!

 Got something to say? Write to us at editor@craftzine.com.

Susie Bright
Susie's Home Ec

» Susie Bright is an amateur dressmaker and a professional writer.
She blogs at susiebright.com.

Stash: Confessions of a Fabric Addict

Before I started sewing, I thought a "stash" was a secret bag of illicit drugs. An ounce of pot, two tabs of something psychedelic, the hash oil lint from a Navajo rug ... that's a stash.

Now that I have an attic, a closet, and the entire floor under two beds crammed with my guiltiest pleasure, I know differently. Fabric, not weed, is the devil's worst temptation: those silks, crushed velvets, buttermilk knits, and bouclé remnants, the cashmere lengths, the chiffon waves. I'm helpless.

I have enough patterns and fabric to clothe the world, open a retail emporium, hoist a circus tent. It's still not enough for me: "My name is Susie and I'm a stashoholic." My hoard of yardage makes my entire lifetime of prescription, over-the-counter, and recreational drugs look like a pitiful bump.

This is how it started: it was all my daughter Aretha's fault. We took our first sewing class together when she was 10. I knew no more than she did; I couldn't have told you where to plug the sewing machine into the wall.

Aretha took an in-depth look at the pattern books our teacher offered us. "Let's make mommy and daughter dresses that match!" she said. She was mesmerized with one of those McCall's Stepford duo photographs of a mother clutching the hand of her daughter, both in identical pink shifts, like Balthus meets Barbie. What empty-eyed phonies!

But when your child asks you, with stars in her eyes, if the two of you can make matching costumes, to parade through the streets as perfectly synchronized beloveds, you know what happens? You tear up, you clap your hands with joy, your voice scales up a full octave: "Oh goodie, let's do it!"

We started combing through the color-fields of cotton prints at our local fabric shop. Aretha pulled out a bolt of tropical and dark green forest leaves,

against a black background — a jungle print with a hint of abstraction. I loved those colors, too. "Let's get six yards!"

But then, shouldn't we also have a Plan B, in case we screw up our first pattern? Or what if we change our minds in the middle of the night?

After all, there was a whimsically *Eloise at the Plaza* print of pink poodles and Eiffel Towers that caught my eye, which I immediately dubbed French Bitch. I can't resist a fabric with a sense of humor — one of my favorite dresses is made from something called Rocket Rascals: an Apollo-11-era design of little boys and girls running around the ether in naughty space suits.

The two of us took no chances; we got everything: the fabrics for Plan A, Plan B, and Plan C. My teacher applauded our choices, as did all the other students. It's like being in a bar at 6 a.m. with all your friends. Have another one!

Now there *are* sensible reasons why serious sewers have to accumulate fabric faster than they can sew it. First off, *you are dealing with limited quantities of unique designs that often cost a small fortune.*

If you can get lightweight sky-blue linen that feels like heaven in your hands for under $10 a yard, you *have* to buy it, even if your sewing machine hours are booked up until the Rapture. You are quite right to think you will never see a deal like that again.

Then, there's the serious sewer's tool chest. You're going to need silk, cotton, and rayon linings in neutral colors — there's no escape from it. If you buy a pattern simply because it has a unique scalloped collar on an otherwise plain bodice, you're saving yourself many hours from drafting that collar yourself. And it's uncanny how scallops work their way into your life! You *do* need tulle — you can't get through the holidays without it. You'd better grab it in turquoise, as well as the ivory and black. You need

Illustration by Samantha Hahn

velcro fasteners, 20" zippers in every shade, and polar fleece in every solid color. You do.

What is the most frivolous fabric in my stash right now? That's hard to say. My sweetheart just started working in hospitals, where he wears scrubs, and he noticed that other nurses and techs show up in all kinds of prints. The traditional pale green and blue are completely out of fashion today on the ER floor — you've got to express yourself! There's a great Kwik Sew scrubs pattern that has pockets galore, so I made him an offer: "I'll get some cotton prints that'll make you proud, and your patients happy."

This is what I came home with: *Brokeback Mountain* cowboys striking poses against a rodeo background. It's cotton! It's apparently from a whole line of Village People prints of hunky dudes vamping around in blue-collar poses. The store was sold out of the construction workers print, and the firefighters. I bought the last five yards of do-me cowpokes they had left!

Can Jon wear this to work? Probably not, though I swear it'd give his terminal patients a well-needed laugh. Does he still want me to make them up? Hell yes! He'll be able to dine out in this outfit for years.

What's the most expensive unused fabric I have in my stash? Italian cashmere, embroidered charmeuse silk, and some crazy scarlet faux lamb fur that seemed critical one winter. I haven't used them out of sheer intimidation: "I can't screw this up, it's so expensive; one day I'll be 'good enough' to take scissors to it."

Rationally, I take a dim view of these excuses. If I buy it, I need to have the nerve to cut it out. I learned that lesson after two years. All my most ridiculous purchases were made when I was a new sewer, and my eyes were bigger than my stitches.

Organizing fabrics and patterns is the first sign to the stashaholic that they are unequipped for their addiction. I literally put a floor in my attic to hold my inventory. But how to organize it all? I've photographed it, labeled it, and alphabetized — cut out samples and stapled bits to index cards with cunning descriptions. But my attempts to act like I'm a lady of leisure who can spend every waking hour running a fabric museum are a joke. When push comes to shove, you'll see my legs sticking out from under my bed, stuffing in another Trader Joe's grocery bag of unmarked yardage.

My general system, which has survived my folly, is to use file drawers for patterns. Since most of my work is digital now, it freed up a lot of hanging file folders for my precious out-of-print Vogues and Christine Jonsons. For fabrics, I separated the wovens from the stretchies, the linings and the novelties, the cottons from the wools, and it really helped. It's grotesque to go through 40 boxes to find one Hawaiian print that burns in my memory, but I can go through two or three.

I took myself off email lists for sales at Jo-Ann's and other fabric stores. I don't let myself web-browse at Emma One Sock unless I'm really sick in bed with the flu. Until I've made pajamas for everyone in the Yukon Territory, I am not allowed to buy another inch of flannel, not even the French Bitch.

I remember the innocence of the mother-daughter outfit days. When we put on our leafy-green shifts, people gasped: "Oh my god, you're wearing matching marijuana-leaf dresses!" I put my hands over Aretha's ears and shot them a dirty look. We picked our jungle print in the purest spirit of color appreciation and delight at the artist's tropical spell. It felt great in our hands. We thought we looked so cute. No one can ever take that away from us. ✄

✚ Check out related links from this story at craftzine.com/08/bright.

CRISPY

Tinsnip Sisters

Sisters **Wendy Sumner** and **Cindy Sumner** comprise SisterBloc, a jewelry design and production team based in Tucson, Ariz. The two collect antique cookie and keepsake tins from thrift stores for their line of miniature sculptures in the form of earrings, necklaces, pins, and tiaras.

"What we do is almost like traditional collage, except tin is harder to cut than paper," explains Cindy from the sisters' shared studio, just off the kitchen in her pink and purple adobe home.

Images are cut from the tin using aircraft shears and tinsnips, then are flattened and filed in shoeboxes for later use.

"Pins and big necklaces are much more like a canvas, while the earrings are mostly about color and design and playing with historical shapes," says Cindy, who received a BFA in metalsmithing and jewelry from the University of Arizona. Once the tin is soldered to a brass or stainless steel backing, tools such as a jeweler's saw and bench shear are used for finer work.

The two don't collaborate on pieces but work in tandem, critiquing each other's work and helping one another through creative impasses. Their designs evolve from what Cindy jokingly calls their "genetic aesthetic." The work is suffused with a quirky wit inspired by found images and text — pineapples paired with hearts, skulls dangling from pagodas, and Japanese kanji coupled with Milk-Bone dog biscuits, to name a few.

"One of the things I like about working with a partner is the synergy and silliness that happens," says Wendy, sitting in the spacious sunroom studio crammed with materials and tools.

This silliness is evident in their line of tiaras. The two wanted to do "something fabulous and big and sculptural and fun," according to Cindy. *Jelly-Bean Rain* consists of a little boy in a yellow rain slicker walking through a downpour of jellybeans. "This way you can have your own little wind chime in your brain!" Wendy explains.   —*Katie Kurtz*

≫ **SisterBloc: sock23.com/sisterbloc**

Photography by Sanford Furrow

Temple of Twigs

For two years, an eerie, twisted fairytale dwelling arose from a grassy meadow at the Santa Barbara Botanic Garden. Toad Hall was 27 feet tall, with a domed roof, windows, and doors. It was built entirely of twigs.

"Of course I'm a lightning rod for it," says artist **Patrick Dougherty**, "but people tell me about their favorite sticks and trees all the time."

Who better to tell? He's crafted more than 150 stick sculptures in two decades, and his new works continue to decorate open spaces, indoor museums, and cityscapes in the United States, Europe, and Asia.

Dougherty starts each project with a reconnaissance trip to the site. He soaks in the scenery — nearby trees, architecture, roads — and hunts for sources in the area where he can gather building materials. A willow farm in Pescadero, Calif., offers saplings by the truckload; a swath of logged land hosts plenty of exposed brush ripe for trimming.

"The fact that [the material] comes from the natural world provides a lot of associations for

people — you start reminding them of their place in it and their relationship to it," he says.

Back home in North Carolina, Dougherty sketches. He returns with the focus and determination of a weaverbird, bringing twig after twig together without glue or nails. The wood, he explains, has its own "infuriatingly capable way of snagging."

Sometimes the sculptures are so large that they need added support, in which case he builds scaffolding out of larger branches dug deep into the earth. The works can top 40 feet high and take weeks to complete, but they'll last years if left untouched.

"You see a kid playing with a stick and he knows everything about it," Dougherty says. "He knows it's a tool, a weapon, and a magic wand."

The artist — who's built twig renditions of castles, giant heads, and house-sized teapots — seems to know that sticks can be even more than that.

—*Megan Mansell Williams*

≫ **Dougherty's sculptures: stickwork.net**

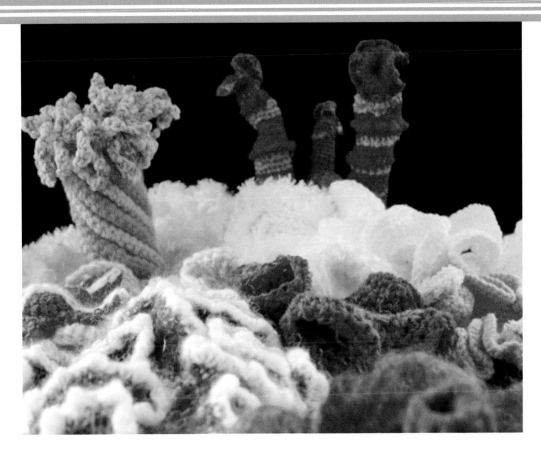

Crochet of the Sea

Photograph courtesy of the Institute For Figuring

While coral reefs are dying out undersea, twin sisters **Christine** and **Margaret Wertheim**, 48, of Los Angeles, are leading a crusade to crochet lifelike coral reefs across America. Their intricately naturalistic yarn reefs draw attention to the threat of climate change, while winning the attention of art galleries.

"They are such fascinating creations," says Christine, who teaches literature and art. But it was a love of math that inspired the reefs.

Co-founders of the Institute For Figuring, dedicated to celebrating the poetic beauty in science, the sisters picked up crochet hooks after studying the aesthetics of hyperbolic geometry.

"We had crocheted some hyperbolic planes which were curled up on a coffee table, when we said, 'That looks like a coral reef — let's make one,'" says Christine. "Two years later, it's taken thousands of dollars and miles of yarn, and we're awash in reefs."

The sisters have crocheted brain, pillar, rubble, and fire corals, forming fluffy ecosystems now teeming with crocheted anemones, jellyfish, nudibranchs, sea slugs, and flatworms — all crafted by applying mathematical algorithms to crochet patterns, increasing stitches with every row.

"Is it art, science, math, or natural history?" asks Margaret, a science writer. "It's all of those things." Each hooked loop is a voyage of discovery. "We are constantly surprised that we set out to make one thing and it turns out quite another. It's evolutionary."

The Wertheims and their collaborators have crafted reefs now exhibiting across America and in Europe: naturalistic reefs in muted tones, others blazing with electric color, and impressionistic reefs that could have lain hidden beneath Monet's water lilies. Their efforts have also spawned new crochet reef projects in Chicago, New York, and London.

"We'd love to inspire every city to create a reef of their own," says Margaret. "There are times when we feel this is taking over our lives. We've become slaves to the reef, like *The Little Shop of Horrors*. Coral has taken over our kitchen, living room, and dining room. Fortunately, we love it." —*Peter Sheridan*

≫ **Institute For Figuring: theiff.org/reef**

Weaver of Illusions

At first glance, **Randy Comer**'s *Bedouin Carpet* leaves you wondering how this weaver has made wool so shiny and rigid. Upon closer inspection, Comer's carpet comes to light as fused glass, a woven illusion that begs touch for proof of medium.

Comer's fascination with glass began more than 20 years ago with a stained glass course at San Francisco City College. Inspired by the stunning painted details of historic San Francisco windows, he studied glass painting and then started enhancing his panels by mixing in kiln-fired components with traditional stained glass techniques.

His current work employs fused glass to evoke aboriginal textiles from around the world. Unlike blown glass, where the artist works with hot, molten masses, fused glass is worked cold. Comer starts by cutting up sheets of colored glass into smaller pieces, arranged together, and kiln-melted into a new unified piece of glass. A single firing takes about 14 hours, and each of Comer's finished pieces requires up to five firings.

Much like traditional textile weaving, at the heart of Comer's technique is geometry, and the limitless idea that all kinds of designs can be made with straight-line segments. The glass he uses is ⅛" thick (think of that as the weft). The smallest piece that he can cut with a traditional glasscutter is ¼" wide (the warp). And together, when melted just right, the glass seeks its preferred thickness of about ¼".

"If you start graphing designs with multiples of these dimensions, it all starts looking pretty familiar. The ancestors have been down this path over and over."

Textiles are just the starting point for his design inspiration. Comer seeks to offer his own modern interpretation of ancient artifacts. "Baskets and mats are among the earliest utensils/tools developed by people. I see my work as a riff on life's basic necessities — amplified and decorated, but still just a tray or a basket."

Comer weaves history and medium, technique and design, bringing the modern and traditional full circle, all while pleasantly defying expectation.

—*Goli Mohammadi*

≫ **Comer's glass: randycomer.com**

Photograph by Sam Murphy

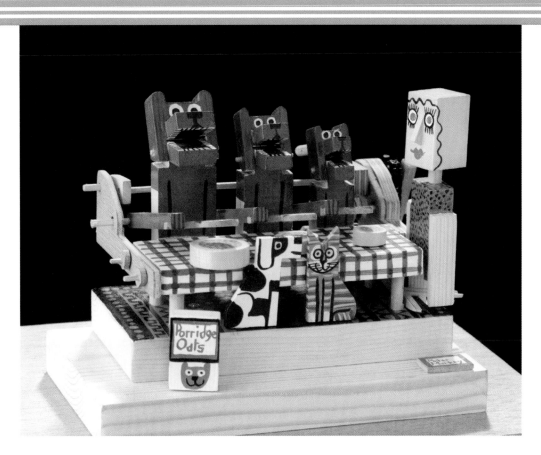

Photograph courtesy of Lacey Jane Roberts

Turning Heads

Art moves people — or rather, people move art, if **Peter Markey** has anything to say about it. For years he's been building his automata: brightly colored and minimally carved wooden figures rigged with handmade cranks and gears, waiting to be brought to life. At the turn of a wooden dowel, two statues side by side become lovers stealing a kiss, or a boat moves across wooden waves.

Markey says his childhood belonged to a different era. "There was no television," he says. "The time was filled with made-up games and making things."

Girls knitted and crocheted, and boys had hobbies. Even then, Markey was drawn to wood, carving pipes for his father, egg cups for his mother, and toy soldiers for himself. Raised in wartime England, he understood the value of using what you had.

Now a retired art teacher in his 70s, slightly deaf and ill-disposed toward computers, Markey's subjects have developed along with his style. His current project is a series of figures inspired by global warming, featuring pedal-powered helicopters and one- or two-wheeled cycles. He also fashions paper cutout versions of his models — right down to paper gears — giving non-mechanical-minded folks a chance to build automata of their own.

He's never claimed to be a master craftsman. In fact, he does as little carving as possible; his models abound with straight lines, triangles, and rectangles. He chooses only soft woods, so that all he needs to do is cut the pieces to size for arms, legs, boats, and birds. Then he paints everything in bright colors, as a rebellion against a time when plain wood was all the rage. The end result is a 3D masterpiece, anywhere from 2 inches to more than a foot high.

For Markey, it's all about design. "Art, like everything else, is solving problems," he says. "The main question is, what can I leave out? What is the simplest and easiest solution?"

—Nellie McKesson

≫ **Paper automatons:** opticaltoys.com/markey.htm
≫ **Peter Markey Exhibition:** focsle.org.uk/first/markey
➕ **Markey's works in action:** craftzine.com/08/handmade_markey

Ulla-Maaria Engeström
Linkages

Ulla-Maaria Engeström lives in San Francisco and is CEO of Social Objects, Ltd., founder of Thinglink (thinglink.org), and author of the HobbyPrincess blog (hobbyprincess.com).

Big Returns

If a crafter or designer takes as her mission the making of durable products that resist fast-changing trends, can she succeed in business without having to sell her principles? This spring Marimekko, the original 1960s "slow fashion" brand, entered into a controversial deal with H&M, the ubiquitous mass-producer of disposable clothing, addressing just this question.

I've been a loyal Marimekko fan for more than a decade. I fell in love with their colorful textiles and founder Armi Ratia's commitment to creating elegant and timeless garments. For me, Ratia's mission materialized in two stunning dresses my mother wore in the 60s.

These days I wear those same dresses, and look forward to passing them on to the next generation. The age-defying dresses stand testimony to the success of Marimekko's slow style, an antithesis to the wasteful seasonal fashion rally.

When H&M announced in November that it would be using classic Marimekko prints and models as a source of inspiration for its 2008 spring and summer collection, Marimekko's customers predictably cried foul. Why is the company that Michelle Lee likened to McDonald's in her book *Fashion Victim* suddenly so interested in slow fashion? Because *vintage is hip*.

In return for letting H&M reinterpret its products and image, Marimekko got its brand name and logo to be the central focus of H&M's global advertising campaign, sweeping over bus stops and billboards from Shanghai to San Francisco like graffiti written in disappearing ink.

Marimekko's former CEO Kirsti Paakkanen (she has since stepped down) explained that the partnership "considerably increases Marimekko's visibility among the young fashion-conscious consumers." As a result, one of the world's biggest marketing engines is currently promoting everlasting Marimekko as this summer's trend.

Not everyone chooses the route that Paakkanen

EVERLASTING TREND? Marimekko meets H&M.

chose for Marimekko. Some years ago I interviewed the founders of ten highly regarded niche design brands for my master's thesis. In every single company, the growth of the business had flattened when it reached a yearly income of $3 million. Surprisingly, the reason for their stalled growth was not that there wasn't more demand for their products.

Instead, the owner-CEOs simply did not want their companies to grow any bigger. They didn't want to compete on price; they were committed to making the highest quality products. And this, putting quality before profit, was how they had managed to create the classics that collectors paid top dollar for at auctions and vintage markets. Things whose makers are known for their commitment to quality don't lose their value. On the contrary, like good wine, their value grows over time.

It has become a phenomenon of its own that big retailers like H&M hire celebrities like Viktor & Rolf, Karl Lagerfeld, and Madonna to design special collections. These collections have been very successful, and people of every age are thrilled to dress like movie stars at an affordable price.

But will these mass-manufactured celebrity designer items hold their value? Will some of the H&M clientele, the friends of fast fashion, turn into fans of slow fashion? Or will trend-conscious consumers soon think Marimekko is *so* out of season? ✕

Photograph by Sam Murphy

Crafting without Scissors

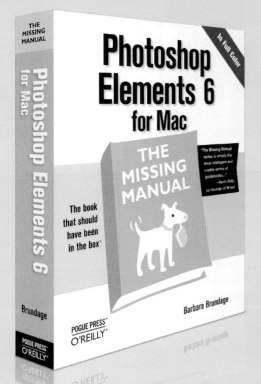

You know that Photoshop Elements can turn casual snapshots into top-notch photos. But do you realize how much *else* you can do with this program? From gentle introduction to sophisticated tips, this bestselling Missing Manual helps transform your pictures into stunning scrapbook pages, calendars, slideshows, and much more.

"I don't do manuals! Which is why I was surprised that a book titled *Photoshop Elements 6 for Mac: The Missing Manual* was so easy to read. Can I see myself using this book many, many times? Definitely! I've already got a forest of stick-it notes bristling out of its pages. If you've bought Photoshop Elements 6, I recommend you check out this book."

**—Karen Bellamy of Scraps of Mind
www.scrapsofmind.com**

Photoshop Elements 6 for Mac
by Barbara Brundage
ISBN 978-0-596-51936-0, 554 pages
$44.99 US / $44.99 CAN
March 2008

Photoshop Elements 6 for Mac: The Missing Manual is the only Elements book available written just for Mac owners. Whether you're scrapbooking, sprucing up your photos, or even creating digital art projects from scratch, this Missing Manual is your best friend for answers.

Visit **www.oreilly.com** today and buy any two books—you'll get a third one free! Just use the discount code **opc10**.

THE MISSING MANUALS
The books that should have been in the box

**POGUE PRESS™
O'REILLY®**

OUR FAVORITE TRINKETS & TREASURES

1. Pulp Fiction

Look twice at these lush bouquets and you'll see Jude Miller's expert hand at work. Each petal and leaf is fashioned from paper to sweetly cheat the seasons. judemiller.com

2. Chaos Theory

Contemporary artist Mia Pearlman explores "the picture beyond the big picture" with her cut paper installations. Intricate shapes conjure up both the weightlessness and the dramatic power of cloudscapes, bringing the heavens down to Earth. miapearlman.com

3. Practical Magic

Have you ever stopped a moment in the middle of crafting, mesmerized by the perfect curl of a pencil shaving or twist of a measuring tape? Victoria Mason understands the impulse, and creates fantastic jewelry for the thoughtful crafter. victoriamason.com

4. Mad Platter

Pairing water-jet technology with classic ceramics, Australian artist Mel Robson creates porcelain silhouettes from platters, with a modern eye for shape and texture. Happiness may be a warm gun, but this is one cool dish.
feffakookan.
blogspot.com

5. Pop Opulence

Jared Brown's densely wrought embroidery captures amazing pop culture moments, from the Avengers on the go to David Bowie's pensive pout, and imagines others, like Mr. Spock in a psychedelic rainbow shower.
craftzine.com/go/
jaredbrown

6. I, Dragonfly

Possibly the most expensive item on Etsy, this exquisitely crafted mechanical dragonfly proves that robots can be beautiful.
jessedanger.etsy.com

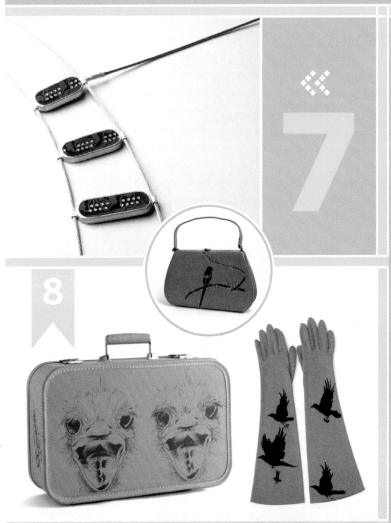

7. Circuit Beauty

Shining a spotlight on technology's hidden building blocks, Susannah Dwyer's earrings, necklaces, and cuff links made from circuit boards extend the life of parts we rarely see. susannahdwyer.com

8. For the Birds

Liz Saintsing repurposes vintage accessories with clean, modern silk-screened designs. If Tippi Hedren had been wearing these gorgeous pink gloves in *The Birds*, she might have had an easier time of it. lizsaintsing.com

9. Lino Block Party

Time to rethink linoleum floors. Forget the school cafeteria; Laurie Crogan sees bright geometry and intricate art deco inlay instead. She cuts linoleum, vinyl composition tile, and cork into one-of-a-kind floors. Her passionflower inlay will put spring in your steps. inlayfloors.com

10. Lovely Letters

Love is blind, says Jessica Lertvilai, so she takes love letters and transcribes them into Braille. Her stunningly minimalist vase ends up as "both a coded pattern and an abstract pixelated painting." supermarkethq.com/product/135

11. Double Muumuu Happiness

These reversible (yes, reversible!) purses come in many shapes and sizes, are tastefully colorful, made of repurposed Hawaiian fabrics, and look fantastic. What's not to like? denisetjarks.com

12. Felt So Good

Felt's sculptural possibilities are pushed to the outer boundaries with Stephanie Metz's soft yet decidedly uncuddly needle-felted creatures, from the hyper-realistic *Jackrabbit* to the darkly hilarious *Teddy Skulls* series. stephaniemetz.com

CRAFTER

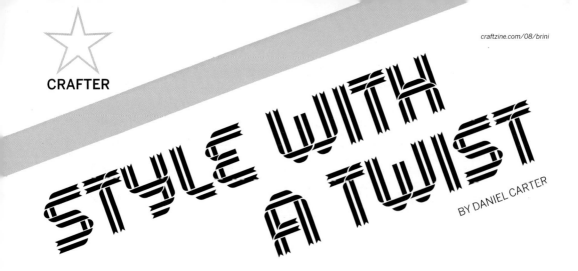

STYLE WITH A TWIST

BY DANIEL CARTER

Wry humor and a healthy dash of know-how help Brini Maxwell serve up her smartly designed, 1960s-inspired décor.

Brini Maxwell is a character fabulously frozen in a scene from a cocktail-fueled 1960s home décor show that never really existed, but should have. Not as blue-blooded as Martha Stewart or as innocent as Doris Day, Maxwell is her own entity: the star of her own TV show and the creator of podcasts, a book, and a new line of home products.

Maxwell, aka actor Ben Sander, is a graduate of Fashion Institute of Technology and a former fashion designer. She launched *The Brini Maxwell Show* on public-access cable TV in 1998, shooting the show in her own meticulously retro apartment.

Picked up for two seasons by the Style Network, the show is a laugh-out-loud romp, ironic yet full of useful tips, from crafts to cocktails to cooking. Currently on hiatus, Maxwell can be heard on her regular NPR podcast, *Hints for Gracious Living*, and all her TV episodes are transcribed at her website, brinimaxwell.com.

Maxwell's current project makes her signature look available to all: a line of colorful, mod-inspired home décor goods called Felix Populi (felixpopuli.com). The shop features an expanding selection of home furnishings, table linens, and a daisy embroidery kit inspired by what she calls the "elegant embroidery designs of the 60s and 70s." Looking like something straight off the set of *Bewitched* or *That Girl* (two of her many inspirations), the colorfully quirky products reflect the same sense of style and humor found on Maxwell's show.

DC: What led to your first cable-access show?

BM: I was decorating my apartment to look like a 60s movie set, right down to the utilitarian stuff like mixing bowls. I found a sensational set of vintage Pyrex ones at a thrift shop and was very pleased with myself, until I realized that they would never be seen. When I had people over they'd be tucked away in their little cabinet, so instead of having an emotional crisis I decided to do a television show with a cooking segment in it. That way everyone could see those great mixing bowls.

DC: Crafting is a big part of your show. What are some of your favorite projects, and how did you originally get interested in crafting?

BM: I really enjoy the process of making things. It's very therapeutic. I enjoy sewing and needlework as well as graphic design (arguably more of an art than a craft, but it informs most of the projects I do). Some of my favorite quirky crafts include artificial fruit made from sewing trims and styrofoam forms, charm bracelets featuring fobs made of beads and head pins, and the wonderful world of tassels. ✄

➕ Read more of our interview with Brini Maxwell at craftzine.com/08/brini.

Daniel Carter is creative director of CRAFT.

RETRO QUEEN: Brini savors a delightful cocktail in her stylish Chelsea apartment, surrounded by Felix Populi pillows, coasters, and embroidered creations.

CRAFTER

LOCAL GIRL COMES HOME AND MAKES GOOD

BY ANNIE BUCKLEY

Utilizing talent from her small-town community, Natalie Chanin grows her line of fashion and homeware.

When Natalie Chanin left Florence, Ala., at the age of 18, she headed first to New York, then to Europe, working as a costume designer and stylist for the fashion and entertainment industries. Twenty-two years later she returned to Florence to make hand-stitched T-shirts with the help of local seamstresses.

Her small line of shirts met with big success, and eight years after her return, Chanin remains in Florence as her expanded collection takes off. Her clothing sells to high-end stores such as Barneys in New York, but each garment is made — from start to finish — right at home.

Chanin's commitment to using local labor was instigated by necessity. "I couldn't find anyone in New York who could do this kind of work!" she says of the complex needlework necessary for pieces like a handmade, painted corset with sculpted flowers or a reverse-appliquéd dress.

Her line has expanded to include handmade jewelry, 100% organic textiles, and home furnishings, such as barn chairs refurbished with woven seats and quilts embellished with appliquéd flowers, all with Chanin's trademark blend of old and new.

While her handmade T-shirts were capturing the attention of the fashion elite around the world, her hometown was suffering the effects of multiple factory closures and job losses.

"We are not solving the economic problems of the region," Chanin concedes. But her company, Alabama Chanin, is based on a cottage industry model in which local sewers essentially own their own businesses and set their own hours.

"We do the designs and sales in-house ... and then the sewers choose which designs they want to make, purchase the raw materials from us, and turn around and sell us the finished goods," she explains.

"People ask me if I'm an activist, and I guess I have become one on a grassroots level," she says. Chanin's business model is not accidental. In 2006, she and her former business partner parted ways. Chanin experienced the pain of company closure so common in her community, and came to the conclusion that "a big part of design is the product, but another part is the kind of company you have."

Determined to create an environment where "everybody in the company has to win," Chanin is as passionate about protecting the environment as she is about local labor, heirloom sewing techniques, and great design.

To make her designs accessible to a wider audience, Chanin co-wrote the *Alabama Stitch Book* (Stewart, Tabori & Chang, 2007) with journalist Stacie Stukin. Chock-full of tips and advice, the book includes instructions for 20 projects. "If you can't afford to buy a corset from us," Chanin says, "hopefully you can afford to buy the book and make it yourself — or hire someone in your community to make it for you." ✄

Annie Buckley is a writer and artist living in Los Angeles. Read her stories on anniebuckley.com.

Photography by Robert Rauch

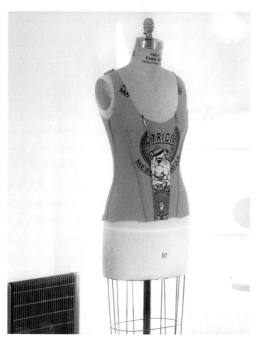

★ RIGHT AT HOME:
Above, the T-shirt corset and rag boa are projects found in the *Alabama Stitch Book*. Below, Chanin relaxes at home.

Spynning STORIES

BY ANNA DILEMNA

A new invention records sounds, images, and more onto knitted objects.

Knitters indulge in their craft everywhere. They knit while chatting with friends, while waiting for the train, during family parties, and on camping trips. Oh, the stories those knitted pieces could tell, if only they could speak.

In fact, that just might be possible. The idea — to imbue knitted objects with the memories and stories that unfold as each piece grows stitch by stitch — is one objective at the Center for New Media at the University of California, Berkeley. Professor Kimiko Ryokai and graduate student Daniela Rosner have devised Spyn, a system that allows knitters to incorporate photos, videos, sounds, and time and place data into their pieces.

"When I knit something, all the places I go and the things I experience become a part of that object, but I never felt that those things were available to the person I gave it to," says Rosner. "We decided to create Spyn so that knitters would have a way to provide a connection between the physical craft and the story that went into its making."

Here's how Spyn works. Attached to the knitter's basket or bag is a knob called the rotary encoder and a small mobile computer equipped with a camera, a GPS tracker, and a touchscreen display (it looks sort of like a large iPhone). As the knitter knits, yarn that has been printed with invisible infrared ink patterns is pulled through the encoder knob, which keeps track of exactly how much yarn has been used. At any point while knitting, the knitter can stop and use the camera to record sounds, take a photo, or make a video.

When finished, the knitter points the infrared-enabled camera at the knitted object, and on the screen one can see pointers indicating all the places where data was recorded. The computer does this by reading the invisible ink patterns, then correlating them with the encoder data on how much yarn has been used. One simply has to touch the pointers to play back the videos, photos, or recorded sounds and see when and where they were captured.

> *"We decided to create Spyn so that knitters would have a way to provide a connection between the physical craft and the story that went into its making."*

As part of their research, Rosner and Ryokai enlisted 12 knitters to try Spyn out. One knitter (their names are withheld due to their roles as participants in a study) decided to use Spyn to incorporate the process of baking cookies into a scarf she was knitting for her brother. She took pictures of the recipe and made videos of herself talking as she knitted and baked. "I loved the idea of giving a present that contains so many layers," she says. "In addition to giving him a scarf, I could also give him a window into my life."

Another knitter used Spyn to keep records of how she resolved various technical challenges in a scarf she knit for herself. "As a knitter who likes to alter

Spinning a Yarn: *Spyn creators Professor Kimiko Ryokai (right) and grad student Daniela Rosner (left) demonstrate how Sypn works while weaving a tale of the demonstration at the same time.*

patterns, start projects without patterns, and teach herself new techniques, I think the record-keeping possibilities of Spyn are a great learning tool," she says. "I'm also excited about the idea of producing a web-based gift along with the knit that includes a slide show with captions, music, or the sound-scape of the knitting experience and GPS-generated maps of where I was and the paths I traveled during knitting."

The name Spyn comes from the storytelling expression "spinning a yarn." Knitting and storytelling have always been linked, and this is reflected in the huge popularity of online knitting communities such as Ravelry and the thousands of knitting blogs where one can read about such varied topics as cable stitches, teething babies, and vacations gone awry all in a single paragraph.

Rosner and Ryokai hope to one day make Spyn compatible with websites such as Ravelry, so that knitters can post pictures of their projects that include embedded links to the photos, videos, and sounds that they included in the knitted projects.

Spyn has quite a journey ahead before it's available to the public, but the fact that it's on the horizon is yet another example of how technology can be used to preserve and extend, rather than undermine, the process of handcrafting.

➕ Spyn project website: craftzine.com/go/spyn
➕ Spyn research paper (PDF) by Rosner and Ryokai: craftzine.com/go/spynpdf

Anna Dilemna is a writer and crafter who lives in Madrid, Spain. Her website is annadilemna.typepad.com.

Where Art and Craft
COLLIDE

BY ANNIE BUCKLEY

Contemporary artists use traditional crafting techniques to make their case.

From knitted wall hangings to cast bronze rugs, hand-torched metal to papier-mâché birds, it's evident that crafts inform and inspire a growing number of contemporary artists.

Case in point: the 2007 international art fair Art Basel Miami Beach, where pieces on display included a sculpture constructed from a porcelain animal swathed in a hand-crocheted suit, a painting laced with needlework, a collage bursting with faux flowers and recycled materials, and various discarded soccer balls, bottle caps, and cardboard boxes sewn, glued, welded, taped, or otherwise pieced together with supplies as simple as Elmer's glue and a needle and thread.

Art Basel Miami Beach, the American sister to the main Art Basel show held annually in Basel, Switzerland, draws upward of 20,000 people — artists, dealers, collectors, and enthusiasts from around the world.

A growing number of smaller auxiliary fairs, such as Pulse Miami, Aqua Art Miami, and the New Art Dealers Alliance Art Fair, have cropped up around Art Basel Miami Beach. Works inspired by contemporary crafting — typically found in the free-spirited atmosphere of flea markets or crafting fairs — hold their own in the fast-paced, champagne-laden party scene with price tags that can top $100,000.

"People appreciate something complex and labor intensive, and this is what comes across in these works," says Katrina Traywick, whose Berkeley, Calif., gallery Traywick Contemporary participated in Aqua Art Miami.

Miami's Fredric Snitzer Gallery has participated in Art Basel Miami Beach since its inception. Snitzer notes that young artists are using more of what are traditionally considered to be craft processes. But, he says, "I don't think, in general, that a contemporary artist takes up craft techniques to re-engage in craft so much as that they are open to using anything as a resource for making art. This generation of artists is so hungry to make art that they will take ideas and materials from wherever they need to take them to make their work."

At Pulse Miami, San Francisco's Rena Bransten Gallery exhibited sculptures by Portuguese artist Joana Vasconcelos, who uses handcrafted crochet covers to transform mass-produced porcelain statuary.

At the Aqua Art fair, Seattle's Roq La Rue Gallery took advantage of the setting to display Boo Davis' skeleton-themed quilt draped over the double bed in a room at the Aqua Hotel. As with many of the craft-inspired pieces, this one challenged the familiar borders in the long and complex relationship between art and craft.

"It gets into so many wonderfully murky areas," says Namita Gupta Wiggers, curator at the Museum of Contemporary Craft in Portland, Ore. "But that's what makes it interesting."

Historically, definitions of art and craft have depended heavily on time and place. The evolution of the British Arts and Crafts movement instigated a pivotal convergence in the early 20th century. A renaissance in the use of handicrafts in American art renewed interest during the 1970s. But how do the fields relate today?

"Craft is definitely having a resurgence — it's not a punitive term in the art world anymore," says

Clockwise from top: Elana Mann's *Embroid, Embroil*: needle, thread, yarn, felt, table, and chair, performed as part of *The Other Project* in Valencia, Calif.; Livia Marin's *Ficciones de un uso* (*Fictions of a Use*): wood oval base with 2,200 lipsticks, Santiago, Chile; Bharti Kher's *The Skin Speaks A Language, Not Its Own*: bindis on fiberglass, New York, N.Y.

James Gobel, artist and associate professor at the California College of the Arts.

Howard Fox, curator of contemporary art for the Los Angeles County Museum of Art (LACMA) since 1985, encountered this issue while organizing the 2006 exhibition *Glass: Material Matters*.

"I met artists that didn't want to be included. They seemed to express a bias of elitism that some visual artists have," Fox says. "But I also met those who identify as craftspeople and didn't want their work to be shown in the company of 'highfalutin' sculptors,' specifically those working in a conceptual framework. The bias exists on both ends of the continuum, but as a curator I am more interested in the continuum than in the polarities."

> *"Using techniques associated with craft and decorative arts in an art context doesn't in any way diminish or displace the claims the work can make on our imagination."*

Indeed, one of the artists contacted for this article asked not to be included in a craft magazine. And many artists who employ ceramics or papier-mâché tend not to refer to their work as craft. So while woodworking, knitting, and other craft traditions continue to crop up in contemporary art, these processes are often used in the service of communicating ideas rather than showcasing a process or material.

So what happens to young artists educated in this anything-goes climate — when art is as readily made from cut-and-paste collage as from oil on linen, from recycled tin cans as from cast bronze? Today's art students undergo rigorous critiques questioning everything from their choice of materials and quality of craftsmanship, to the social, political, and other associations their art might suggest.

Elana Mann, a recent graduate of the California Institute of the Arts (CalArts), recalls discussing an artist's work in relation to the role of Michaels stores in the suburban American landscape. "I never grew up with Michaels, but many people talked about how it was their 'gateway' to art-making, or their only outlet as a kid," she says. Mann discovered that crafting "techniques and materials were regarded as merely another strategy amongst a myriad of technical and conceptual approaches artists were using."

When Mann's classmates referred to craft, they typically interpreted the word as recycled containers, glue, and craft store baubles, rather than long-standing customs or apprenticeship. But she took it to another level: Mann used needlepoint, a centuries-old craft, as the basis for a compelling multimedia performance in which she wore an early Colonial dress, stood in front of a stitched mural of the White House, and embroidered an image from Abu Ghraib prison directly onto her hand, letting the gendered history of sewing add layers of meaning to her art.

Perhaps because of the art world's biases against traditional crafts, such as glassblowing and woodworking, a new DIY sense of craft — in the context of reuse and ingenuity — is weaving its way into and becoming more readily accepted in contemporary art than traditional crafts have been.

Fox cites Tim Hawkinson's complex and fantastical sculptures as an example. Hawkinson's widely exhibited body of work includes a larger-than-life organ, pieced together from electrical components and plastic sheeting, and a tiny (and surprisingly realistic) bird skeleton sculpted from fingernail clippings.

"It is extraordinary sculpture, but is also heavily freighted with subtext and context," Fox says. "His work is profound, but he uses extremely simple, hobby-like construction techniques, hardly more complicated than Tinkertoys or putting something together with velcro. The fact that he uses simple techniques and humble materials doesn't diminish the work in my mind. Using techniques associated with craft and decorative arts in an art context doesn't in any way diminish or displace the claims the work can make on our imagination."

Over the past century, the art object has undergone a historic transformation. From Duchamp's famous challenge to art in the form of a urinal in 1916, to the conceptual art movement spurning the art object altogether in the 1960s, the way something is made — or crafted — is expected to inform the concept behind the work. Most artists use craft, or any other process, be it manufacturing, painting, or digital media, as a means of communicating ideas.

"An artist might work in the tradition of needlework in order to talk about the complex range of ideas associated with this tradition, either to comment on it ironically, to quote it, or to use these same skills to refute the very biases associated with them," says Elizabeth East, managing director of L.A. Louver Gallery in Los Angeles.

The meticulously crafted sculptures and collages

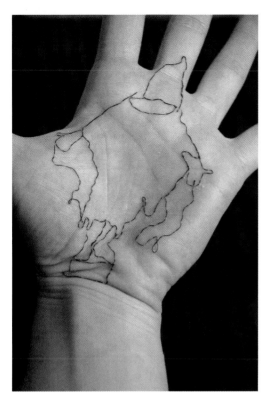

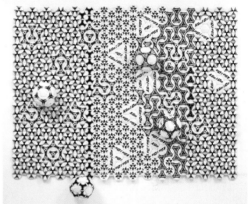

Photography (clockwise from top left) courtesy of Scott Groller; by Tamara Weikel; courtesy of the artist; and Sara Meltzer Gallery; by Boo Davis/Quiltsrÿche

of Bharti Kher, on view at Art Basel Miami Beach in conjunction with New York's Jack Shainman Gallery, are covered with row upon row of bindis, small stickers deriving from a Hindu tradition of painting a red dot on one's forehead. The spiritual, cultural, and philosophical significance of this material adds multiple layers of meaning to Kher's works, which include large sculptures of a heart and an elephant, furthering her visual exploration of immigration, identity, and cross-cultural movement.

In the elephant sculpture, Kher uses snake-shaped bindis and "places them in circular patterns, as if they were hair or fur, and they give the work texture," says Stefania Maso at Jack Shainman Gallery.

Even as this level of elegance in fusing craft and concept has become a standard-bearer, another kind of work is putting process at the center. Livia Marin uses a lathe to carve lipsticks into small sculptures that she carefully installs, by the thousands, into complex ribbons of color. Although her work relates to constructed ideas about glamour and consumerism, the visual fascination of a labor-intensive process like Marin's takes precedence over material associations, challenging the now-established hierarchy of concept over craft.

But that's the beauty of art: as soon as you think you have it figured out, something changes, definitions shift, and a new range of possibilities emerges.

Clockwise from top left: Elana Mann's hand embroidery of an Abu Ghraib prisoner; Mandy Greer's *Small But Mighty Wandering Pearl*: wood, cloth, papier mâché, steel, fabric, yarn, glass, glass and plastic beads, wool, plaster; Felipe Barbosa's *Three-dimensional Opp Ball*: sewn soccer balls; and Boo Davis' *Pieces of Mind* quilt (Roman Stripes variation).

Annie Buckley is a writer and artist living in Los Angeles. Her writing appears regularly in *Artforum*, *Artweek*, *A&U*, and other publications. She enjoys discovering art that will appeal to CRAFT readers. anniebuckley.com

Button Rings BY JODIE CARLETON

❖❖ Want to showcase the beautiful old buttons in your collection? These button rings are an easy way to adorn your fingers with the stray stunner that stole your heart.

YOU WILL NEED:

» **Ring findings** I use the adjustable sort with a perforated disc or screen, used to make beaded rings, found at bead supply shops.
» **Embroidery thread or dental floss**
» **A selection of buttons** Flat or sew-through buttons work best, but you can also use small shank buttons.

1. Choose your button(s).

If you want to stack your buttons, you can sew them together before attaching them to the finding. Sew through them once or twice and tie a firm knot on the underside. I used a mixture of vintage and new buttons.

2. Sew your button(s) to the finding.

Sew right up through all the button layers if possible, lining up the holes as you go. If you can't sew through the buttons, just sew the disc to the buttons by passing the needle through the knot on the underside. Sew them on firmly, and tie off your threads at the back or weave them back in under the disc to hide the ends.

3. Slip on your ring.

Show off your bling! When you get bored with the buttons, you can just snip them off the disc, return them to your stash, and make some new rings.

Jodie Carleton is a try-anything-once crafter whose recent exploits include resin casting, tissue felting, and mural painting. She blogs about her crafty adventures at vintagericrac.blogspot.com.

Photography by Sam Murphy

Craft:  WEAVING

What do glass, wool, and electronics have in common? Each is a medium used in weaving, as we'll show you in these pages. You'll also learn about the origins of this ancient craft, how to build and use a loom, and how to make cool woven stuff. Plus, we give you a FREE mini loom that will demystify the process and fire you up to get started!

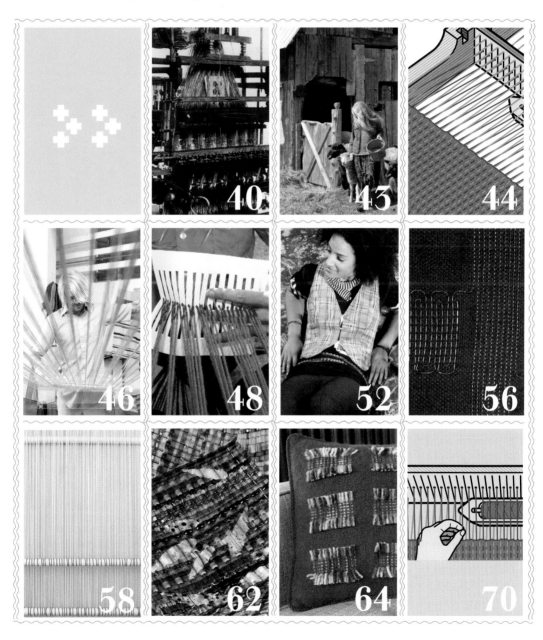

40

43

44

46

48

52

56

58

62

64

70

Weaving Through the Ages

A SHORT HISTORY OF WEAVING AND HOW IT INFORMED THE CREATION OF EVERYTHING FROM CLOTH TO THE COMPUTER.

BY LIZ GIPSON

Weaving has occupied the human experience since practically the dawn of human existence. There is no known record of the first weaver, or why she decided to weave. Perhaps she observed birds making nests or spiders weaving webs, and decided to mimic the patterns she observed in nature, making a basket to carry food from one place to another by gathering and interlacing reeds.

The first physical evidence of woven cloth was found in a burial ground associated with the ancient Greek colony of Pantikapaion, now the modern-day city of Kerch in the Ukraine. It is believed that these fragments date back to the fourth millennium B.C.

Ancient mythology abounds with references to weavers and their cloth. Spider Woman — not the Marvel comic book character, but the Navajo deity considered the original spiritual weaving teacher — is said to have provided the thread that drew the Diné, or Navajo, from the third world to the fourth, the world of time and physical being. Scholars believe that the Navajo people learned to weave from the Puebloans sometime in the 16th century.

In Greek mythology, the peasant Arachne believed she could weave better than the gods.

Athena, the weaver among the gods, was offended by Arachne's boasting, challenged her to a weave-off — and lost. Athena humiliated Arachne and drove her to take her life, but later, showing remorse for her behavior, she revived Arachne and changed her into a spider.

Some of the earliest documented accounts trace the origin of ceremonial Kente weaving to early traditions in the West African kingdoms that thrived between A.D. 300 and 1600. The Ashanti, who live in what is now Ghana in West Africa, are known for their mastery of this colorful, strip-woven cloth. According to legend, the first man to weave — it was mostly men who wove for centuries — learned the art by watching a spider at work.

Weaving as Necessity

Throughout history, most people knew how to weave. In fact, until the Industrial Revolution — the great divider between the time when we knew how stuff was made and modern times, when most don't have a clue — people made their own clothes, or at least participated in some way in making them (buying the cloth from a weaver, taking it to a seamstress,

Protection

FOR THE

INDUSTRIOUS

Weavers.

INFORMATION having been received that a great number of industrious Weavers have been deterred by threats and acts of violence from the pursuit of their lawful occupations, and that in many instances their Shuttles have been taken, and their Materials damaged by persons acting under the existing Combinations :

Notice is hereby Given,

That every Protection will be afforded to persons so injured, upon giving Information to the Constables of Stockport: And a Reward of

FIFTY GUINEAS

Will be paid, on conviction, to the person who will come forward with such evidence as may be the means of convicting any one or more of the offences mentioned in the Act of Parliament, of which an Extract is subjoined : And a Reward of

TWENTY GUINEAS

Will be paid, on conviction, to the person who will come forward and inform of any person being guilty of assaulting or molesting industrious and honest Weavers, so as to prevent them from taking out or bringing in their Work peaceably.

PETER BROWN, ⎱
Stockport, June 17th, 1808.   T. CARTWRIGHT, ⎰ CONSTABLES.

By the 22nd, Geo. 3, C. 40, S. 3.

It is enacted," That if any person enter, by force, into any House or Shop, with intent to Cut and Destroy any Linen or Cotton, or Linen and Cotton mixed with any other Materials, in the Loom, or any Warp or Shute, Tools, Tackle, and Utensils, or shall Cut or Destroy the same, or shall Break and Destroy any Tools, Tackle, or Utensils, for Weaving, Preparing, or Making any such Manufactures, every such Offender shall be guilty of FELONY, without Benefit of Clergy"

OPPOSITE: In legend, the spider taught African weavers, who today create brilliant Kente cloth. LEFT: English police offered rewards to catch rebellious Luddites. TOP: Gandhi's wife taught him to spin. He encouraged Indians to weave rather than buy British cloth. ABOVE: Inventor William B. Stout drives the first fiberglass car.

raising sheep, working in cotton fields), not just as a fashion statement but as necessity.

In the early 1800s, a group of weavers near Nottingham, England, did not take kindly to the changes wrought by the Industrial Revolution. With the introduction of mechanization, weavers who formerly worked as independent contractors were driven out of business or forced to work in factories. A guerrilla army of resisters started breaking into factories or using internal sabotage to destroy the mechanized looms. They became known as Luddites, a term we use today to label those who resist technological progress.

Many other expressions also have their roots in woven cloth. For example, before red tape meant bureaucracy, it referred to the handwoven tape, made on small looms and dyed red, that bound official documents from the crown. Revolting against the crown's red tape, both American colonists, and 150 years later native Indians led by Gandhi, refused to buy British cloth that was heavily taxed and instead made their own homespun clothes.

When sailing ships dominated trade — from about the 15th to the mid-19th century — the sails

Until the Industrial Revolution — the great divider between the time when we knew how stuff was made and modern times, when most don't have a clue — people made their own clothes, or at least participated in some way in making their own clothes.

were made by thousands of people spinning yarn, and thousands more weaving the yarn into cloth. Without that cloth, we wouldn't have been able to move anything from one continent to another.

Today, even airplanes rely on weaving technology. Modern structural composites are made by weaving fiberglass and other high-tech fibers, then infusing the web with plastic or other materials to create a lightweight, durable structure for boats, planes, and all kinds of modern vehicles.

Many early manufacturing mavericks got their

FAR LEFT: The Jacquard loom, which used punch cards to store weaving patterns, revolutionized the weaving industry. LEFT: Paper punch cards for computers were modeled after the Jacquard loom's wooden cards. ABOVE: This punch-card reader from the mid-20th century reads data on computer cards, working on the same principle as the Jacquard loom.

start with textile technology. Before Toyota started building cars in the early 20th century, the company built automated looms. The first computer was based on the Jacquard loom, an automated system that used a series of cards with holes punched in them to determine which thread was lifted and which one was not, making it easy to create elaborately patterned cloth with relative ease. This gave rise to the punch-card calculator and eventually those funny cards that were used to run the first computers, which took up an entire room.

Today, we don't weave cloth because we have to; we weave because we want to. Weaving is both a connection to the past and a subversive act, linking us to our ancestors and to revolutionaries. For many, the craft is a rejection of dependence on industrial manufacturing. Learning to make cloth by hand is one way to say, "I can do this myself!"

Liz Gipson is managing editor of *Handwoven*, president of the Spinning and Weaving Association, author of *Weaving Made Easy* (Interweave Press, fall 2008), and the spinning and weaving host of *Knitting Daily TV* on PBS. Needless to say, she is a wee bit smitten with weaving by hand.

The Next Wave of Weaving
What makes weavers giddy these days?

Green yarns Increasingly popular are yarns regenerated from byproducts of natural resources, sold through fair trade, or that are otherwise good for the environment and the people who make them.

Recycled materials Plastic bags, cassette tape innards, rags, and garden waste are all making their way onto weavers' looms.

Shrinking on purpose Making fabric that defies two dimensions is keeping weavers busy, whether it's weaving with yarns that have an extra twist or mixing yarns that shrink with those that don't.

Portable looms From small peg looms that fit in your hand to rigid heddle looms that fold, there are dozens of styles that allow you to weave on the go.

Interiors Weaving for the home — curtains, pillows, rugs, bath towels — can make weavers swoon.

Pattern Fabulous patterning techniques, from overshot to color-and-weave, create cloth that seems complicated but is actually easy and fun to weave.

Lambs to Linens

A SMALL, GREEN WEAVING BUSINESS THRIVES.

BY VICTORIA EVERMAN

Near the border of New York state and Canada in the Adirondack Mountains, Four Directions Weaving is nestled on a quiet country road, more than a mile from the end of the power lines.

When founders Donna Foley (pictured) and Jim Brush bought the property 25 years ago, alternative energy options were still more affordable than trying to connect the abandoned farm to the local power grid. Now, with 12 solar panels and a wind generator, the company is one of the only self-sustaining weaving businesses in the United States.

Foley weaves most of the company's products herself: blankets, rugs, tapestries, and linens. But what sets Four Directions apart from other weavers is the fact that they raise their own sheep, too — a rare breed called Lincoln Longwool. "Raising the sheep is an integral part of the whole weaving process for me," Foley says. "It connects me with weavers and spinners throughout the ages who have been shepherds."

Unlike other lamb breeders who shear the animals' wool in late winter when the temperature can still dip below −40°F, Foley waits until April to shear her flock. She takes advantage of the sun and wind in the spring months to wash the fleece in preparation for the dyeing process.

The rich hues in Foley's work are evidence of her use of natural dyes, which formerly took her up to a month to prepare. "But now, with powdered natural dye extracts, I can get right to the dyeing stage," she says. For those who want to dye their own wool, she recommends extracts from Earthues, a Seattle company that uses sustainably gathered plants, and pays farmers a fair wage for their crops.

Can a green business be profitable? "Having been working 'green' for over 20 years, it is heartening to see it becoming much more mainstream," says Foley. "Before, I almost felt like I had to apologize for using natural dyes. I had to explain my use of organic cotton in baby blankets. Now people come to me for these reasons, looking to have more meaning in their purchases. It is now more viable for me to keep my green commitment."

■ Foley's website: fourdirectionsweaving.com
◘ For more photos, go to craftzine.com/08/fourdirections

Victoria Everman is a San Francisco-based writer, model, environmentalist, crafter, and yogi. Visit her at victoria-e.com.

Photography by Burdette Parks

The Basics of Weaving

BY JANE PATRICK

In weaving, two sets of elements — threads, or yarns, and paper strips, or pliable sticks, for instance — are interlaced. One set, the **warp** (vertical), is crossed by another, the **weft** (horizontal). Together, warp and weft form a woven structure.

The most basic weave, called **plain weave**, is a simple over-under, over-under pattern. From this elementary basis, infinite variations are possible.

Weaving can be done without a loom, as in basket weaving, or with a loom, as in fabric weaving. In either case, the premise is the same: two sets of elements cross each other.

A **loom** is simply a device that holds the warp elements in place and taut, so that the weft can be woven over-and-under across them. A loom can be as simple as a picture frame or piece of cardboard, or as sophisticated as a computer-controlled machine. No matter the style or degree of sophistication, a loom's primary function is to hold the warp. The main difference between a simple frame loom and a complex loom is the amount of work it will do for you.

With loom weaving, the first step is to put the warp on the loom — a process called **warping**. On a frame loom, the warp is placed directly on the loom. More sophisticated looms require more preparatory steps.

Individual warp threads are referred to as **warp ends**, **ends**, or **threads**, and are measured in ends per inch (epi). The weft is the set of threads that cross the warp. Each line of weft is called a **pick** or **shot**. If the weft is yarn, thread, rag strips, or another long, flexible material, it's usually wound onto a **shuttle** for easy handling.

You can pass the weft over and under alternate warp threads one at a time, or you can lift alternate warp threads all at once to make a space for passing the shuttle through. This space is called the **shed**. In a frame loom, a **shed stick** (or **pick-up stick**), a flat stick with pointy ends, is inserted in the shed to hold it open for the shuttle to pass through. The edge of the weaving, where the shuttle exits and then re-enters to return to the other side, is called the **selvedge**. The **fell line** is the last row of weft you've woven in the developing cloth — the place where woven and unwoven warp meet.

THE ANATOMY OF A LOOM

Ⓐ **Shuttle** Holds the weft thread and carries it back and forth through the warp threads.

Ⓑ **Heddle** On a rigid heddle loom, raises alternate warp threads all at once.

Ⓒ **Shed stick** Used with a frame loom, it raises alternate warp threads.

Ⓓ **Warp** The vertical threads on the loom.

Ⓔ **Shed** The space between raised and lowered warp threads.

Ⓕ **Cloth beam or front beam**

Ⓖ **Warp beam or back beam**

Jane Patrick is the author of *Time to Weave: Simply Elegant Projects to Make in Almost No Time* (Interweave Press), on which this article is based. Read her blog at schactspindle.com.

Illustrations by Nik Schulz

On a simple frame loom, a shed stick is used to lift every other warp thread — first one half of the threads, then the other half. In rigid heddle weaving, warp threads pass alternately through slots and holes in a heddle. Raising it lifts half the threads (the ones in the holes), lowering it raises the other half (in the slots). The shuttle carries the weft back and forth.

WEAVING ON A FRAME LOOM

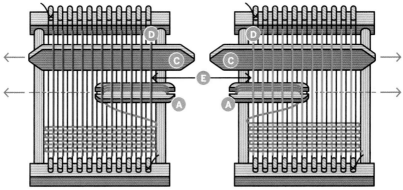

Half of the threads lifted, moving the shuttle from right to left.

Other half of the threads lifted, moving the shuttle back from left to right.

WEAVING ON A RIGID HEDDLE LOOM

Heddle in down position, moving the shuttle from right to left.

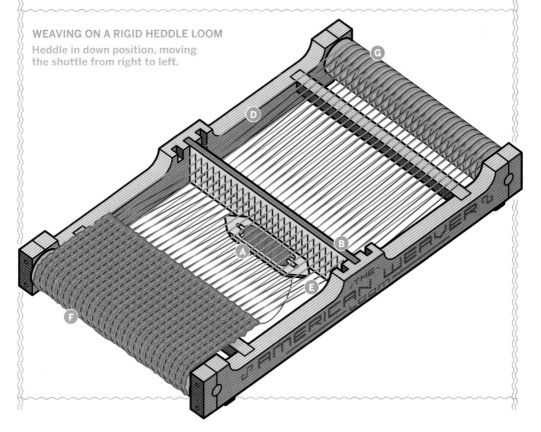

Blanket Offer

A WEAVER GIVES AWAY HIS BLANKETS, BUT WITH SOME STRINGS ATTACHED.

BY TINA BARSEGHIAN

With his ongoing art project *Blanket Offer*, Travis Meinolf attempts to connect the public at large with the ancient craft of weaving in a slightly subversive way. The 29-year-old art school graduate has spent the past year weaving woolen blankets (32 of them) and offering to give them away for free — sort of. He's also designed a pocket-sized, portable cardboard loom that makes it possible to weave cloth just about anywhere.

Tina Barseghian: How did you get started weaving?

Travis Meinolf: My girlfriend at the time introduced me to weaving in 2000. I inherited a floor loom from my great aunt in Wisconsin. We were living with this tool that took up a lot of space, and our choice was either to embrace it, or have it be a white elephant. We started using it and it became a big part of my life. I was seduced by the act, because it was so meditative, and had the end result of producing something. The setup of the loom is where most of the design decisions are made. Once you actually start producing cloth, you're in production mode and not thinking about the design. I like to step in and have it relax me and take away the thoughts of the day.

TB: Why did you design a portable cardboard loom?

TM: The idea behind it is that I can make cloth, and so can you. But people think they have to spend hundreds of dollars on a loom and set aside an entire room in their house to do it. So I wanted to make a loom that I could give out to people, and that's where I came up with the laser-cut cardboard loom that fits in your pocket. I give them away with instructions.

TB: Tell me about your idea of giving blankets away.

TM: I first started weaving blankets with the idea that someone could use it and understand that it was produced by one person's hand. So the idea of producing those first few blankets was that I would offer them freely to anyone who really needed them, rather than give them to specific people or hold onto them. I wanted to brick that hoarding impulse.

TB: Was it hard to give away so many hours of work?

TM: I had to remove myself from the situation. I rented a space in a market at U.N. Plaza in down-town San Francisco and set up a table with three blankets that I'd woven. I put a sign next to it that said: "If you need a blanket to keep you warm, you can have one." I just put them there, and left.

TB: Did you watch to see who would pick them up?

TM: No, I came back when the market was closed. The space seemed well respected. Nothing had been knocked over, and the blankets were taken. The project was complete in my mind. Another time, at a gallery installation, someone said, "I know I don't need a blanket, but how do I get one?"

I didn't sell it to him then, but the next time I had an exhibit, I had the same sign and added, "But if you just want one, you can buy it for $850 as a fine art sculpture." Representing your need versus something you want can happen in the art world. Another time, someone approached me to buy the blanket, and I offered him a DVD that shows him the weaving process. I was attempting to show that it's the labor that gives the objects value. He bought the DVD for $1,500, and got the blanket for free. Once again, it's entirely semantics. He was excited by the fact that I would not sell the blanket but I would manufacture a way for him to have the blanket.

Another project I was working on was to take my floor loom on wheels to street corners, parks, and museums, to show the weaving process and that one person can produce fabric.

TB: How was that received?

TM: Really well. The part that I really enjoy is opening up conversations about textile production that I couldn't have without a loom with me. You couldn't walk up to someone on the street and start talking about the weaving heritage from their country out of the blue. People came up and said, "Back in my country, we would do it this way." Or, "My grandfather did it with goat hair."

Turn the page for a lesson from Meinolf on a specially designed cardstock loom.

Tina Barseghian is editor-in-chief of CRAFT.

Photography by Cody Pickens

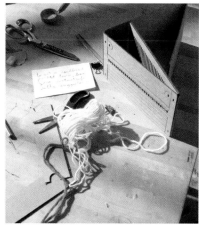

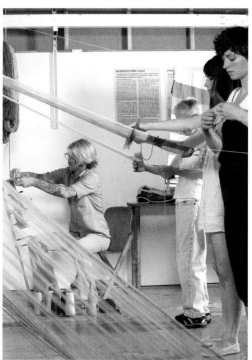

Pocket Power

USE A PORTABLE PAPER LOOM
TO MAKE CLOTH ANYWHERE.

BY TRAVIS MEINOLF

When the inspiration hits to start weaving, pull out your handy pocket loom and you're ready to go. The portable loom is provided here as an insert or online as a PDF at craftzine.com/08/pocketloom.

With the set of measurements in this project, you can easily weave a scarf. For further instruction and other weaving projects, go to actionweaver.com.

MATERIALS

» Scissors or X-Acto knife

» Portable loom

» Pencils, chopsticks, or 8" sticks or dowels (2)

» Knitting yarn

» String

» Fork

Craft:

Weaving is easy! All you need to get started are a few craft-store supplies and this portable pocket loom, designed for CRAFT by Travis Meinolf. With this loom at your fingertips, we hope you'll be inspired to create your own masterpiece. Post photos of your creations at craftzine.com/community.

YOUR FREE POCKET LOOM

Prepare Your Pocket Loom

1. Carefully cut out the cardboard loom and shuttle card, separating them along the magenta lines. Fold the loom on the green dotted line.

2. Use scissors or an X-Acto knife to cut out the gold diamond holes. It helps to cut all the red lines first, then cut all the yellow lines to finish.

3. Now go back across the folded loom, cutting out all the crystal blue slots. When they're removed, unfold the loom.

See page 48 for the full set of instructions.

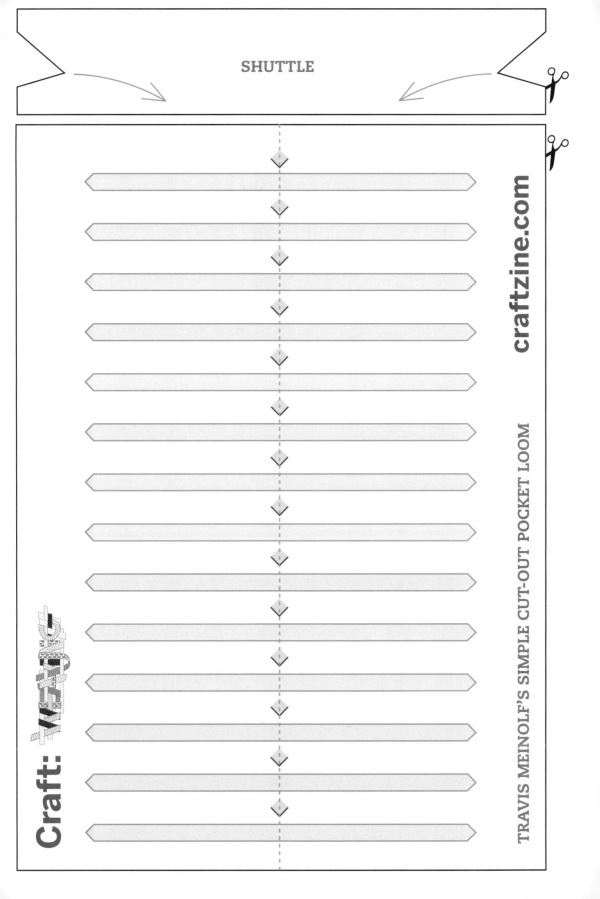

SHUTTLE

Craft:

craftzine.com

TRAVIS MEINOLF'S SIMPLE CUT-OUT POCKET LOOM

Prepare Your Pocket Loom

1. Carefully cut out the cardstock loom and shuttle card, separating them along the magenta lines.

2. Use scissors or an X-Acto knife to cut out the gold diamond holes (Figure A). It helps to fold the loom lengthwise, cut all the red lines first, then cut all the yellow lines to finish (Figure B).

3. Now go back across the folded loom, cutting out all the blue slots (Figure C). When they're all removed, unfold the loom (Figure D).

4. Measure out 28 lengths of yarn by wrapping it around your arm, from thumb to elbow, 28 times (Figure E), then cutting the bundle at the top (Figure F). Thread these 28 lengths through the 28 slots and holes in the loom card (Figure G) and pull them through about 6" (Figure H).

5. Tie the strings you just pulled through the loom card to 1 of the sticks, in bundles of 4 to 7 (Figures I and J). Don't worry about what type of knot — just make sure it's secure.

6. Secure the stick to a wall, table, doorknob, patient friend (I used my own toes), or anything stationary that can handle a clamp, a nail, or more string binding the stick to it. You'll be tugging it hard, so it has to remain steady.

7. Move the loom toward the other end of the strings, working out any tangles as you go (Figure K). When you get close, tie these string ends in bundles of 4 to 7 to the second stick (Figure L). It helps to have a friend hold the stick while you tie the outermost bundles on the far left and far right of the stick. Then, with the outer strings taut, tie the inner ones to match that tension.

8. Use a stronger yarn to tie the second stick to your belt loops or around your waist. Now lean back to hold the threads tight (Figure M). These threads are the warp. The loom card will act as a heddle to raise and lower the warp. You and the materials you have manipulated are now a loom.

9. Cut out the shuttle. Wind another, thicker yarn around the shuttle, in a figure-8 pattern, following

the green arrows (Figure N). This is the weft.

Weave on Your Pocket Loom

10. Pulling back with your body to hold the warp threads taut, pull the loom card upward, so that the half of the warp that's threaded through the golden diamonds lifts above the other half, which should drop to the bottom of the blue slots. The space between is called the shed. Leaving a length of weft hanging off, pass the shuttle through the shed (Figure O). Then use a fork or the loom card to pull the weft toward the stick that you're tied to (Figure P).

11. Continue to hold the warp tight with your body. Reach underneath the loom and pull the loom card downward, so the threads through the golden diamonds dip down below the threads which now rise to the top of the blue slots. Wind more weft yarn off the shuttle, and pass it back through the shed, in the direction from which it came. Again, use the loom to pull the weft toward you and pack it in.

12. Repeat Steps 10 and 11 — you're weaving!

13. When you're done, slip the sticks out, knot the

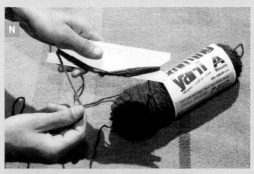

warp threads at the weft edge, and you've got your cloth to do as you wish. This length makes a perfect scarf.

Read about Travis Meinolf in the profile on pages 46–47.

THE LOOM'S EVOLUTION

This cardstock pocket loom is based on Meinolf's original cardboard loom. Using a laser cutter, Meinolf made 50 of the cardboard looms and distributed them at public art exhibitions and at Maker Faire last spring. His goal is to get a loom into the hands of as many people as possible.

Viva la Vest!

MAKE YOUR OWN FABRIC USING KNITTING YARNS.

BY JOAN SHERIDAN HOOVER AND BECCA OLSEN

The rhythm of weaving is soothing, and creating your own fabric is addictive. Weaving is easy (remember those potholder looms you used as a kid?) and you can do it with things you probably already have around the house. We raided our knitting stash for yarns and used a scrap of plywood and a box of nails to make the loom.

For this project, we used plain weave — over 1 thread, under 1 thread. By using different yarns to provide color and texture, you can achieve great looks with this simple fabric structure. We ended up making a vest with our woven fabric, with the help of a commercial sewing pattern.

Joan Sheridan Hoover (a weaving shop owner) and Becca Olsen (a high school student) are weaving buddies who enjoy playing with yarn. For local weaving resources, visit the Spinning & Weaving Association at spinweave.org.

Photograph by Cody Pickens

MATERIALS

» **Commercial sewing pattern with recommended notions**

» **Yarn**

» **Lightweight fusible interfacing**

» **Cheap wooden rulers (2)**

» **Paint stirrers, well sanded (2)**
These are your shed sticks.

» **Fine sandpaper**

» **Plywood board** at least 1" larger than the piece to be woven

» **3d finishing nails, 1¼"**

» **Hammer**

» **Pencil**

» **Straightedge**

» **Measuring tape/ruler**

» **Scissors**

» **Masking tape**

Calculating How Much Yarn You Need

By doing a bit of math, you can easily calculate how much of each yarn you need.

Warp Count Take the total number of nails on your loom and multiply it by the distance in inches between the 2 rows of nails. Divide by 36. Our warp used 96 nails and measured 30" long (96"×30" = 2,880" and 2,880"/36 = 80yds).

Weft Calculate the weft as the same quantity of yarn as the warp, and you'll have plenty.

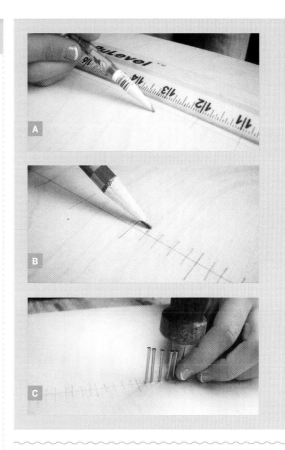

1. Build the loom.

1a. Determine the size of the loom you need by measuring your pattern pieces and adding 20% to the measurements to allow for shrinkage, etc. Add 3" to the length for loom waste. When you measure the pattern piece, make sure to take into account the grain line, as this can change the dimensions.

1b. Transfer the dimensions to the plywood board using a measuring tape and straightedge. We made parallel lines 11" long and 30" apart. Mark the lines in 1" intervals, making sure the marks are square to the marks on the opposite end (Figure A).

1c. Subdivide each 1" segment by making tick marks to measure off $^1/_5$" (Figure B), or 5 threads per inch. Eyeballing it is fine. If you use bigger yarn (worsted or bulky weight), measure ¼" segments (4 threads per inch).

1d. Pound a nail ¼" into the board wherever the tick marks intersect the line (Figure C).

2. Begin to warp.

2a. Tape the end of the starting yarn to the board as shown in Figure D, and thread it past the first nail. Wind the yarn to the corresponding nail on the other side, from right to left. Take the yarn back to the starting side and wrap the next nail from right to left. Continue. Push the yarn down against the board as you go, maintaining light, even tension.

2b. If you want stripes, add a new yarn by taping it to the board. (The previous yarn can be carried on the outside of the nails until it's used again.) When you're finished with a yarn color, cut and tape it to the board. Continue until all the nails are used up (Figure E).

3. Make a shuttle.

We used 1 shuttle for the main color and 1 shuttle for the plaid colors. We found that shorter shuttles worked best because of the relatively small amount of yarn used, especially in the plaids.

If you don't have access to pre-made shuttles, you can easily make one. Use a box cutter or X-Acto knife and cut a cheap wooden ruler to the desired length. If weaving with only 1 color, make your shuttle 1" wider than the warp width. Carve out a notch at each end, and use sandpaper to smooth out rough edges (Figure F).

4. Weave.

4a. Wind your shuttle using a figure-8 pattern on both sides of the shuttle, as shown in Figure G.

4b. Tighten the warp tension using a binder or other found objects (Figures H and I). The amount of tension needed will change as the project pro-gresses — when the warp is too tight, change to a shorter tensioning object.

4c. Insert a paint stirrer (your shed stick) by going under alternate threads (Figure J). For example,

warp threads 1, 3, 5, etc., should be on top of the stick and 2, 4, 6, etc., below the stick. Turn the stirrer on its edge, creating a shed. Work the shuttle through the opening of the shed (Figure K).

4d. Position the weft thread as shown in Figure L, and use the shed stick laid flat to beat the yarn into place.

4e. Slide the first shed stick to the top of the binder. Create a second shed using another paint stirrer with threads 2, 4, 6, etc., on top (opposite the first stick). Turn the second stirrer on its side to create the second shed, insert the shuttle (Figure M), beat the yarn into place, and remove the second shed stick. Bring the first shed stick forward and weave as before.

4f. Continue weaving by using the "stored" shed for the first pass and creating an opposite shed anew each time for the second pass.

NOTE: Since the side selvedges won't be used in the final piece, if you need to insert or drop a yarn, just leave a tail at the edge (Figure N).

5. Finish.

5a. To remove your fabric from the loom, cut the ends (Figure O) long enough to tie knots to secure the final rows (Figure P). Lift off the nails on the end where you began weaving (Figure Q).

5b. Hand-wash the woven pieces in the sink, squishing them around a bit. Lay flat to dry.

5c. Trace your pattern onto fusible interfacing, noting the grain line (Figure R). Follow the interfacing's instructions to adhere it to the back of the woven fabric (Figure S). Match the pattern's grain line with the direction of the warp. Follow the pattern's steps to sew the vest.

Photograph by Cody Pickens (T)

Completing the Circuit

LAURA MacCARY MAKES WEAVING INTERACTIVE.

BY SYNE MITCHELL

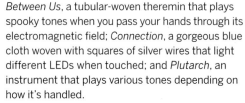

Laura MacCary's work explores our relationship with aspects of life so pervasive we overlook them: textiles, electronics, trash, even the lowly cockroach. Her work combines fiber arts and electronics to draw out the extraordinary in the everyday.

"I'm interested in how we interact with technology," says MacCary, 41, of Tacoma, Wash. "Its fields pass through our bodies — radio signals, cellphone signals, TV — and we never think about them.

"Weaving is another technology that's very intimate and that most people don't think about. I've met people who, when I tell them I weave, say, 'Nobody knows how to do that anymore.' And I say, 'Look at your clothing.'"

The first of four pieces in her *Dialectric* series, *I and Thou* is a 25" square of cloth woven from ¼" reel-to-reel audiotape. When you touch it, your skin completes a circuit and it generates a series of clicks. The pitch and rate of the clicking vary with the surface area of skin that you press against the cloth. *Dialectric*, which has shown in one California and six Washington state galleries since 2002, is a play on words — a combination of *dielectric*, a nonconductive material used in electronics, and *dialectic*, a logical discussion.

While the piece was on display, people responded to the circuit in intimate ways, pressing their faces, hands, or forearms against it, trying to get new sounds. They reacted to it as if it were an interactive entity instead of an object.

"When I saw people interact with the prototype, I got excited," MacCary says. "We, as humans, anthropomorphize everything. I was interested in that."

A malfunction in the electronics of *I and Thou* caused MacCary to seek technical support from her father, Lawrence MacCary, a lifelong electronics tinkerer who lives in Spokane, Wash. This led to additional collaborative pieces in the series: *The Space*

Between Us, a tubular-woven theremin that plays spooky tones when you pass your hands through its electromagnetic field; *Connection*, a gorgeous blue cloth woven with squares of silver wires that light different LEDs when touched; and *Plutarch*, an instrument that plays various tones depending on how it's handled.

MacCary's most recent work, *Nest*, appeared in the Seattle Dorkbot exhibit *Strange Things*. Inspired by a set of antique candy molds, MacCary cast three fist-sized bug bodies in crystalline sugar. Embedded inside each is an electronic circuit that causes a red LED to glow and pulse in a heartbeat rhythm when you lift one from its red satin nest. "I wanted people to consider the fact that even a cockroach has a heart and can be sweet," MacCary says.

MacCary's 500-square-foot studio is an enviable treasure trove of eclectic materials. "It increased my productivity when I was able to get everything out of boxes in the attic," she says. "Now I look at my stash every day and that sparks ideas."

On her loom now are feather-boa-like scarves woven out of cassette tape discarded by a local recording company. Loops of black-and-brown film rustle like a living thing when you pick one up. Part garment, part Slinky, it's almost impossible to put down.

What lies in the future for this champion of overlooked wonders? MacCary is currently taking sewing classes, with an eye toward producing art garments. Her first impulse: to make jeans. Once again, elevating the everyday.

Syne Mitchell is the editor of WeaveZine (weavezine.com), a new online magazine for handweavers, and also produces a monthly podcast, WeaveCast (weavecast.com). She is a weaver, science fiction writer, and former physicist.

Photography by John Keatley

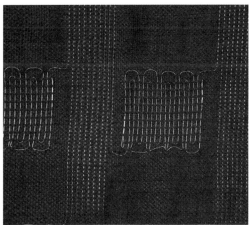

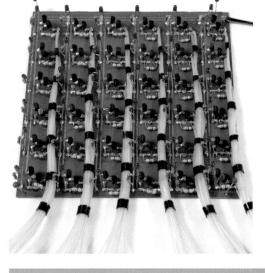

FACING: Detail of *Connection*. TOP: Laura MacCary holding *Huggable HAL*, flanked in the background by *I and Thou* (left) and *Connection* (right). The artist is wearing a hand-woven boa made from recycled cassette tape. CENTER LEFT: Detail of *Connection*, showing the wire woven into the fabric of the cloth. CENTER RIGHT: Detail of *Connection*, showing the circuit board and LEDs. BOTTOM: A cast-sugar bug from *Nest*.

Weaving on the Go

BUILD YOUR VERY OWN LAP LOOM
AND WARP IT TOO!

BY KRISTIN ROACH

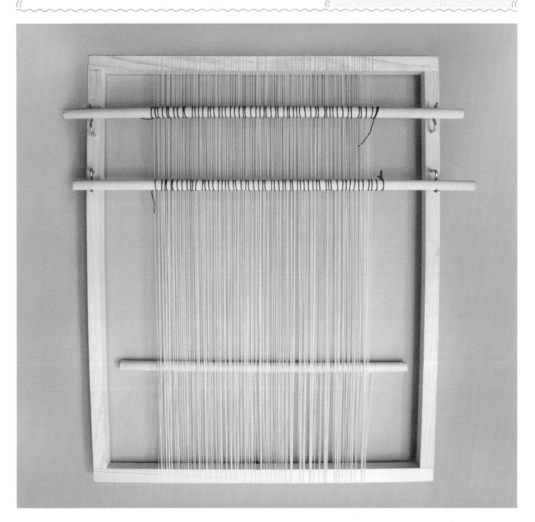

I have wanted to weave since I can remember, but I always thought it was impossible because of space constraints. Then I got my hands on a tapestry loom!

With a tapestry loom you're able to weave the full length of warp because it's wrapped around the frame. You actually shift the warp bar, and therefore the warp, around the whole frame. So even though the loom is only 22" tall, you have 40" of workable warp! With the use of 2 heddle bars, it's easy to open up 2 sheds for all sorts of tapestry weaving adventures. The materials cost less than $20, and it takes about 20 minutes to make the loom's frame and then 2 to 3 hours to warp it.

Kristin Roach enjoys finding purpose in forgotten materials and experiences. Her work ranges from painting to pattern writing. kristinroach.wordpress.com

Photograph by Sam Murphy

FOR THE LOOM:

» **Uni-Stretch embroidery frame stretcher bars (2 pairs) sizes 22" and 18"** available at Michaels. You can also use canvas stretcher bars in the same sizes, available at your local art store; just make sure to pick up 2 of each size.

» **½"×36" wood dowel rods (2)**

» **⁹⁄₁₆" screw hooks, 2" long (4)**

» **Wood glue**

» **Drill and small drill bit**

» **Pliers**

» **Bench vise**

» **X-Acto knife**

» **Small saw** for cutting dowel rods

NOTE: You can make your loom any size. I have looms ranging from 8"×10" to 18"×22"; just remember that if you go larger than that, you need to build your frame from wood that is at least 1"×2½" or the tension of the warps will, well, warp your frame. I have even snapped a few frames, not a fun experience at all.

FOR WARPING:

» **100yds of sturdy yarn** Cotton size #10 works well. Warping yarns have to be of a particularly hardy breed. A good test is to hold a length of yarn in your hands and pull; if it holds, then it should be just fine. You want something that will make your hands hurt when you try to break it.

» **20yds of sturdy yarn in a contrasting color**

» **1"×18" strips of cardboard (2)**

» **Sheet of paper**

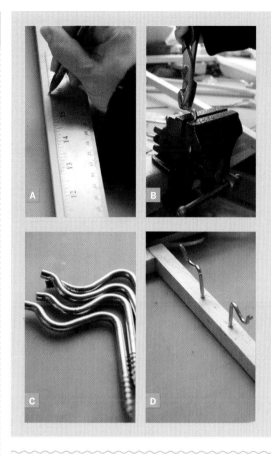

1. Build the loom.

1a. Fill the joins of your frame with glue and snap them together. This usually requires the gentle nudge of a floor or a rubber mallet.

1b. On your frame, mark where your 4 screw hooks will go. Mark the 16" and 18" points on the long sides (Figure A). Drill the 4 holes just deep enough to get the screws started, ¼" or less.

1c. Bend your screw hooks over backward. Clamp the screw end into your vise, with the open part of the hook facing toward you. Grab the end of the hook with your pliers and bend it away from you until it is parallel to the floor or as close as you can manage (Figures B and C).

1d. Twist the screws into your starter holes (Figure D).

1e. Cut your dowel rods by clamping them in your bench vise. You need 2 lengths of 20" and 1 length

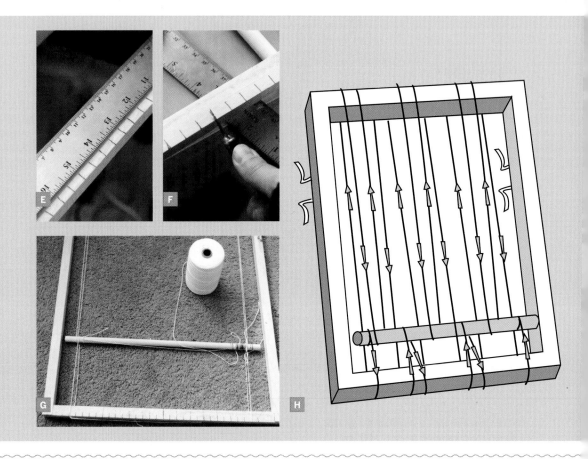

of 16". The latter is your warp bar; it needs to be able to fit inside your frame.

1f. Measure out every ½" across the top and bottom of the front side of your loom. Start by finding the center, and mark every ½", working your way to the outside of the frame (Figure E). Make sure you mark the center so that it stands out a bit.

1g. Make notches at every ½" mark, using your X-Acto knife; just score the frame lightly (Figure F).

NOTE: The front of your loom is the side with the modified screw/hooks in it.

2. Warp your loom.
2a. Tie temporary supports to your 16" warping bar, the bar that shifts your work around the frame. This bar needs to be positioned in the bottom quarter of your frame. Secure the warp bar by tying yarn to both ends and then to the top of your frame.

Repeat, this time tying the bar ends to the bottom of your frame. Adjust the temporary supports until the bar is parallel to the frame and is held tight (Figure G).

NOTE: When planning your project, you may only want an 8"-wide piece. Measure 4" to either side of your center point so it will be nice and even. I went for the full 16" this time around. Remember, though, that the wider the piece, the longer it will take to warp.

2b. Tie 1 end of your warp to the left side of the warp bar, where your piece will start. For an 8" wide piece, you would tie it 4" to the left of the center point of your warping bar. You'll also want to think about how many warps per inch you want. For our project we'll use 10 epi (ends per inch). We marked off every ½" with a score mark, so we just need to make sure we get 1 warp into each score and 4 in between.

Illustration by Kristin Roach

2c. For the warping pattern, you need to go down and around the bottom of the loom from back to front, up and over the top on the front side, down and around the bar on the back side, up and over the top on the back side to the front, around the bottom to the back, around the bar, and repeat from the beginning until you have the right amount of warps. Just tie off your warp end to the bar. If you're a visual learner, this diagram with fancy arrows will totally help (Figure H). Here is my warping in progress, about 4" into the 16" (Figure I).

3. Make the heddles.

3a. First you need to make sure your warps aren't crossed. The best way to do this is to weave one of your cardboard lengths through the warps by picking up every other warp. Then pick up the remaining warps with the second piece of cardboard.

NOTE: It's clear when the warps aren't lining up correctly and you need to re-pick some warps so they're in the proper order. If a warp crosses, it's much easier to fix now than later.

3b. Place a 20" dowel rod into the lower pair of screw hooks and tape it in place. This is your bottom heddle bar. Using your cardboard as a guide, slip the leftover 16" dowel into one set of alternating warps. This is your shed or pick-up stick. Scoot it so it's directly below the bottom heddle bar.

3c. Tie the end of your yarn to the bottom heddle bar and start looping the warps to the bar. Bring the yarn under the warp, over the bar, and back under the bar, through the loop you just created, and down to catch the next warp (Figure J). Continue until you have picked up all the warps, and tie the end of the yarn to the heddle bar.

3d. Repeat Steps 3b and 3c for the second, top heddle bar and the other set of alternating warps. Now you're ready to start weaving (Figure K)!

The Glass Weavers

MARKOW & NORRIS RAISE THE MELTING POINT WITH THEIR GROUNDBREAKING SCULPTURES.

BY ARWEN O'REILLY GRIFFITH

With formidable technical skill and a keen eye for color, Eric Markow and Thom Norris (wovenglass.com) have spent the past five years doing the impossible: they've developed a technique to literally weave glass.

The Falls Church, Va., artists create both fantastical and abstract works that revel in the rich, luminous properties of glass. From the enormous Peace Crane to smaller, more intimate tabletop works that invite you to peer into them, Markow and Norris prove that you don't need a loom — or even fiber — to weave.

Arwen O'Reilly Griffith: What are your backgrounds? How did you get involved with glass?
Eric Markow: B.S. in chemical engineering.
Thom Norris: B.S. in biology. We met in early 1994, and Eric had started taking a class in stained glass at a local community center. I started working with Eric on small projects and slowly they turned into larger projects and commissioned works around the Washington, D.C., area. We created very abstract, organically inspired stained glass windows for the next decade.

Photography by Javier Agostinelli

AG: When and how did you start weaving glass?

EM: In early 2002, we bought our first kiln with the intention of making our own flat glass panels to include in our stained glass windows. One of our original concepts was to make a glass panel look like a basket. We made some strips of glass that had different-colored lines in them. We cut them into squares and alternated them into a checkerboard pattern. From a distance it looked woven, but up close it was obvious that an actual weave eluded us.

So we spent several years and hundreds of experiments learning how to actually weave different colors of glass with different temperatures together.

AG: What were some of the logistical and technical challenges you came across?

TN: Eric's technical engineering side gave him the patience during all the experiments; I was more frustrated during the process because I just wanted to make something. We found out that all the colors of glass had a range of melting temperatures. Additionally, not all the colors of glass are compatible and they may not stick together during the weaving and firing process.

To make matters more complicated, we weren't satisfied with the limited colors available in commercial sheet glass, so we started making our own signature colors, [which] also had different melting temperatures and needed to be tested for compatibility.

AG: What do you love about weaving glass? What do you think is the most interesting aspect?

EM: We try to take our sculpture beyond the weave technique itself. We use the woven glass literally as fabric to create the various sculptural shapes that amuse and inspire us. We strive to make sculptural shapes that have a "wow" factor from a distance, but we love that the woven glass reliably provides an additional "wow" factor upon close inspection.

TN: Many people still can't believe it is woven glass until they touch it. We do encourage touch, since we have worked very hard to maintain a very textured surface. This too is challenging; if we heat the glass too much it will simply all run together and become a smooth surface. We say we have to keep it at the "taffy" stage, not the "honey" stage.

AG: Do you set out with an idea to start, or see how the piece evolves?

EM: Sometimes we have the concept and overall shape drawn out first, and create the colors to fit our needs. Other times we create a bunch of beautiful color samples while testing temperatures, and the colors tell us what they should become. Some

LEAVES OF GLASS: The natural world comes right into the gallery with *Box of Koi* (left) and *Saguaro* (right).

sculptures are named first and created later, others are created and sit in the studio or our home for quite some time before we name them. We try to create a theme each year to add continuity to the new sculptures; this year the theme was Japanese origami.

TN: The theme helps us focus the hundreds of ideas that are bouncing around in our heads. There are sculptures that we have been thinking about for years that just don't seem to be ready to make. Sometimes our own growth with the technique helps us flesh out sculptures that we previously could not physically create.

AG: Are there new developments in store, or are you still enjoying the challenges you currently face?

TN: We want to take our sculpture to a grander scale. We are very inspired by the American painter Georgia O'Keefe and we love her concept that if you want people to look at something, make it big.

➕ For the full interview, go to craftzine.com/08/markowandnorris.

Arwen O'Reilly Griffith is staff editor of CRAFT.

Fringy Loom-Woven Pillow

PRACTICE USING A RIGID HEDDLE LOOM
AND WEAVE A COLORFUL CUSHION.

BY JANE PATRICK

For the budding weaver, a rigid heddle loom is affordable and easy to use. To make this woven pillow, you'll use one color of yarn for the threads on the loom (the warp), and another color to weave with (the weft).

To accent your pillow you'll use a bundle of 4 colors and a pick-up stick. If you've never woven before, weave the back of the pillow first. By the time you finish the back, you'll be ready to tackle the front using 2 shuttles and a pick-up stick.

This is a perfect first project. The thick wool yarns weave up quickly, and the colorful fringe accent adds a bit of zest and is easy to accomplish.

Jane Patrick is the author of *Time to Weave: Simply Elegant Projects to Make in Almost No Time* (Interweave Press), and the sales and marketing director for Schacht Spindle Co., Inc. Get Schacht's weaving patterns at schachtspindle.com.

Photograph by Sam Murphy

MATERIALS

» **Rigid heddle loom with a 20" weaving width** I used Schacht Spindle's Flip Folding Loom that comes with a 10-dent reed (to yield 10 threads per inch), a warping peg, threading hook, and 2 stick shuttles.

» **Pick-up stick**

» **Cascade 2-ply merino wool yarn** (1,000yds/lb) available in 3½oz, 220yd skeins, in the following colors:
  » **Dark red-orange, color 2425 (2 skeins)**
  » **Burnt orange, color 9465B (2 skeins)** used for the warp
  » **Dark green, color 2445 (1 skein)**
  » **Medium green, color 2429 (1 skein)**
  » **Light green, color 8903 (1 skein)**
  » **Bright yellow, color 7827 (1 skein)**

» **Heavy paper** such as grocery bags

» **Fiberfill stuffing** like Poly-fil, or Nature-Fil, made from bamboo and organic cotton

» **¾" velcro strip, about 5" long**

» **Muslin or scrap fabric** to make the inner pillow

» **Sewing machine or hand-sewing supplies, and scissors**

» **Incredible Rope Machine (optional)** from Schacht Spindle. I used mine to make a twisted cord finish, but you could hand-twist or braid a trim.

» **Warp length: 2½yds** allows about 30" for loom waste and practice

Width in the rigid heddle reed: 19"

Warp ends per inch (epi): 8

Number of warp ends: 152

1. Thread (warp) the loom.

Your warp (the threads that run vertically on the loom) will be 2½yds long.

1a. Place the warping peg in front of the loom, 2½yds away from the back apron rod.

1b. Clamp the loom to the table, with the back of the loom hanging over the edge of the table, and place the burnt orange yarn on the floor underneath the apron rod. Facing the back of the loom, tie the yarn onto the rod close to one end (it doesn't matter which side, whichever is most comfortable for you).

1c. Using the threading hook, take a loop of the warp yarn through the slot in the heddle (½" from the edge of the heddle) and carry it over to the warping peg (Figures A and B, next page). There will now be 2 warp ends through the slot.

1d. Bring the yarn around the apron rod and through the next slot, and then around the warping peg (Figure C). Continue in this manner all the way across your loom for a total of 19" (152 ends). Tie off the end on the apron rod (Figure D).

1e. Cut the loop of warp yarn around the warping peg and tie it in 1 big, loose overhand knot (Figures E and F).

1f. Wind the warp onto the back beam, separating the layers with heavy paper (Figure G). Check to make sure that the paper is winding on straight. Every so often, pull on the warp at the front to tighten it around the beam.

1g. Turn the loom around and work from the front. Beginning at either edge of the warp, take 1 of the 2 warp ends out of each slot and thread it through the adjacent hole (Figure H). Repeat all the way across until all the holes have been threaded.

1h. Tie the ends in 1" sections (bunches of 8) onto the front apron rod, using the first part of a surgeon's knot (i.e., a double overhand knot, like when you start to tie your shoes but with an extra pass through, as in Figure I). Check the tension all the way across the width of the warp to make sure it's even, then secure the knots with a bow knot (Figure J).

2. Begin weaving.

2a. Wind a stick shuttle with dark red-orange in a figure-8 pattern (Figure K); wind only as much as is comfortable in your hand and will fit through the shed. Place the heddle in the up position and look through from the side; you'll see an opening, the shed, through which you'll pass the shuttle (Figure L). To weave, you'll simply place the heddle alternately in the up position ("up shed") and the down position ("down shed"), passing the shuttle through the shed each time, back and forth.

2b. To spread the warp to prepare for weaving, just pass the shuttle back and forth between the upper and lower sheds 3 or 4 times before pressing the yarn into place using the heddle. Repeat if necessary.

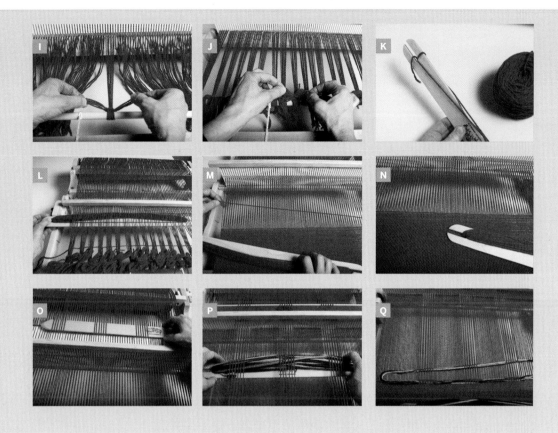

2c. Begin weaving your pillow. Place the heddle in the up shed, insert the shuttle into the shed on one side, and take it out on the other. Press the weft into place with the heddle (this is called beating) and then place the heddle in the down shed and pass the shuttle through the shed to the other side. Beat.

2d. You'll notice that alternate warp threads are lifted each time. This forms the most basic of weave structures, called plain weave. To prevent your weaving from drawing in, run the weft yarn through the shed at a 45° angle before beating (Figure M). Weave so that there are about 8 rows (or picks) of weft per inch. Weave the back of the pillow for 33" and then begin the front (Figure N).

3. Prepare for the pick-up pattern.

Place the heddle in the down shed. Working behind the heddle and using the pick-up stick, count and pick up only the raised warps. Placing a piece of paper between the layers makes it easier to see

what you're doing. Pick up in this way: skip 17 warps, pick up 6, skip 12, pick up 6, skip 12, pick up 6, skip 17 (Figure O). Slide the pick-up stick to the back of the loom until you're ready for it.

4. Weave the front.

To weave the front, use 2 shuttles, one with the same dark red-orange weft you used for the back, and a second shuttle wound with 4 colors for your pattern: dark green, medium green, light green, and yellow (the pattern weft). You'll use the pick-up stick to create the pattern (Figure P).

4a. Weave 2½" in plain weave.

4b. Weave pick-up for 12 rows in the following sequence:
» Heddle in down shed. Weave with burnt orange.
» Heddle in up shed. Weave with burnt orange.
» Place the heddle in neutral, bring the pick-up stick forward to the back of the heddle, and turn the stick

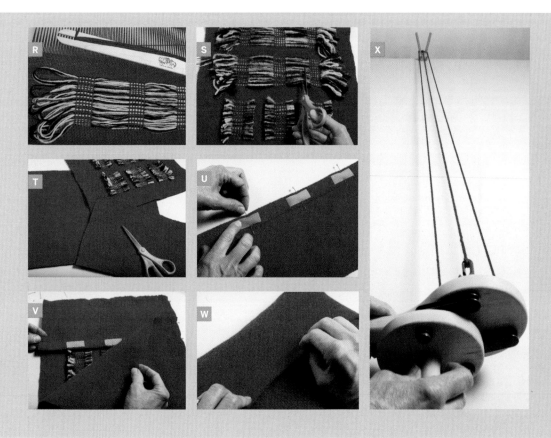

on edge, creating a temporary shed. Now weave with your pattern weft, just in the picked-up warps, leaving a 2" tail at either edge (Figure Q). Return the pick-up stick to the back of the loom.

» Repeat this sequence until you've woven 12 rows of pick-up pattern (Figure R).

4c. Weave 2" plain weave.

4d. Weave pick-up for 12 rows (as in Step 4b).

4e. Weave 2" plain weave.

4f. Weave pick-up for 12 rows (as in Step 4b).

4g. End with 2½" plain weave.

After you've finished weaving, cut the fabric from the loom, leaving long enough warp tails to tie in overhand knots.

5. Wash the fabric.

Machine-wash your newly woven fabric in cold water and detergent, on the gentle cycle. Check the fabric often to make sure it isn't felting too much.

Remove it when it measures about 14½" wide, rinse it in the sink with cool water, and then squeeze out as much water as possible and lay it flat to dry. Your fabric will measure about 40"×14½".

6. Finish and sew the pillow.

6a. Cut the pattern loops and floats (the free ends) to ¾" length (Figure S).

6b. Cut the pillow front, centering the pattern. I measured 2¼" from the edge of the pattern on all 4 sides and trimmed the fabric to this size, creating a rectangle approximately 14" wide by 16" long (Figure T).

Your fabric size will vary according to how much it shrinks during washing.

WOVEN COLOR: The pillow is an easy first weaving project and adds a dash of color and texture to any room.

Photograph by Sam Murphy

6c. Cut the 2 back pieces: a back flap that measures 8" by 16" long (or the length of your fabric) and a back piece 12" by 16" (or the length of your fabric).

6d. On the flap, fold over 1" along a long edge and stitch it down. Cut 3 velcro strips ¾" wide by 1½" long, then center them 1½" apart along the fold and stitch them by hand (Figure U). Use only the hook side of the velcro; it will adhere to the fabric to keep the pillow closed.

6e. To assemble the pillow, place the front piece right side up and lay the back flap along 1 short edge, right sides together and raw edges aligned, with the folded edge toward the center and the velcro facing up.

Lay the back piece along the opposite short edge, right sides together and raw edges aligned. The back piece should overlap the flap by about 2" (Figure V).

6f. Sew a ¼" seam around all the outside edges. Turn the pillow right side out (Figure W).

6g. Make the inner pillow using muslin or scrap fabric. Cut two 15"×17" pieces and stitch them around the edge, leaving about a 5" gap in the center of 1 side. Stuff with polyester fiberfill, distributing the stuffing evenly, and hand-stitch the side closed. Now stuff this inner pillow into your woven creation and close the edge with velcro.

6h. For a professional edge finish, make a 6-strand twisted cord with dark red-orange and burnt orange. To make this cord, I used the Incredible Rope Machine (Figure X) but you could hand-twist or braid a trim. Hand-sew the cord around the edge of the pillow, tucking in the ends.

Weaving: Where to Begin

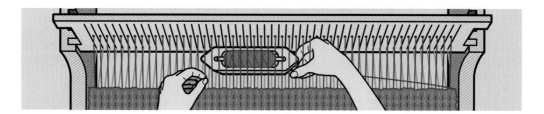

LOOMS & SUPPLIES

Schacht Mini Loom Weaving Kit
$32

halcyonyarn.com/kidstuff.html

Beginning weavers can learn how to weave their own bags, mats, coasters, and more with this portable weaving kit. The plastic mini loom comes with 2 shuttles, a beater, weaving needle, five colors of yarn, and project instructions. Perfect for kids!

Webs
yarn.com

Webs' online store carries a multitude of weaving resources, from looms and tools to a variety of weaving yarns including alpaca, bamboo, silk, and more.

BOOKS

Learning to Weave
By Deborah Chandler $28

learntoweave.com

Considered to be one of the best books on the basics of weaving, *Learning to Weave* is now the de facto standard textbook for weaving teachers. You'll learn the basics of weave structures and weaving tools, how to warp, and how to read and design drafts.

Handwoven
$7, or $24 subscription for 5 issues/year

interweave.com/weave

Handwoven is a seasonal magazine for the weaving enthusiast that covers a variety of weaving projects and how-tos. Check out their website for great weaving resources and bunches of free projects.

ONLINE RESOURCES

Spinning and Weaving Association
spinweave.org

Download the Spinning and Weaving Association's brochure "Get Weaving!" for a great weaving introduction. The website also provides a list of local shops and other resources such as lists of weaving teachers and events.

Handweavers Guild of America
weavespindye.org

Finding a weaving guild will prove to be invaluable during your weaving journey. The Handweavers Guild of America maintains a list of guilds in the United States and Canada, and abroad.

WeaveZine
weavezine.com

WeaveZine is a seasonal online magazine that features weaving projects, product reviews, and how-to videos.

WeaveCast
weavecast.com

An audio podcast and blog for handweavers, WeaveCast features interviews with weaving specialists and authors.

Ravelry
ravelry.com

And, yes, popular social networking sites such as Ravelry have weaving threads, too. Check them out — you're bound to find a weaving friend near you.

Compiled by Liz Gipson and Natalie Zee Drieu.

Illustration by Nik Schulz

Craft:
PROJECTS

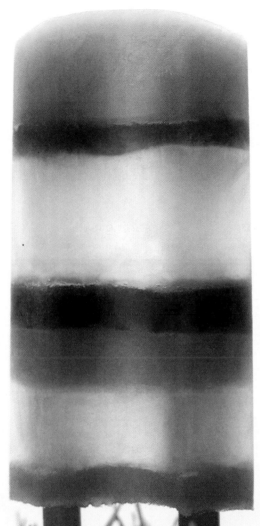

Photograph by Emily Brooke Sandor

Summer days are meant for serious self-indulgence. To that end, we offer you a way to savor the season: the perfect ice pop, with instructions on how to make your own ice pop molds. Inspired by the warm weather, we give you a pattern to make a modular fair-weather dress, ruffles included. And for those who want to create their own exterior view, there's a tutorial on making beautiful stained glass windows.

POP STARS

By Krystina Castella

MAKE YOUR OWN CUSTOMIZED MOLDS AND REFRESHING ICE POP INGREDIENTS TO GO IN THEM.

»» In the height of summer, there's nothing like an ice pop to cut through the heat. Though store-bought ones do the job, pops made by hand — both the molds and the juicy refreshers — will taste that much better.

» Eleven-year-old Frank Epperson invented the Popsicle in 1905 when he left his fruit-flavored soda out on the porch overnight with a stir stick in it. He patented the idea 19 years later.

Ice pops can be cast in any shape you envision. You can make simple pop molds from everyday household items or from food packaging. If you want to get really crafty, you can experiment with liquid silicone and make your own mold.

» Building a log cabin is a popular popsicle-stick craft for kids.

You'll find these instructions and recipes, as well as many more, in *Pops! Icy Treats for Everyone* (Quirk Books).

» Former Hollywood stuntman Robert McDonald created a working replica of a Viking ship using 15 million recycled popsicle sticks to show children that anything is possible.

Photograph by Emily Brooke Sandor; illustrations by Tim Lillis

Krystina Castella is an industrial designer who designs environments, furniture, clothing, stationery, housewares, toys, and cupcakes. She is a professor at Art Center College of Design in Pasadena, Calif. icypops.com

WHAT YOU'LL NEED

[A] Paper or plastic cup or food container or cardboard to construct a box

[B] Food-safe liquid silicone and catalyst I use Silpak R-2237-SL liquid silicone, but there are many other options available online.

[C] Found object, or object sculpted from clay, wood, or wax

[D] Container for mixing silicone

[E] Rubber bands

[F] Hot glue gun and glue sticks

[G] Utility knife

[H] Uncooked rice

[I] Gaffer's tape or duct tape

SCARED OF SILICONE?

Look around the house, and you'll notice a slew of other options.

» Paper and plastic cups

» Snow cone wrappers

» Aluminum foil muffin cups

» Shot glasses

Pops can be served in the mold or removed before serving. Consider the presentation possibilities and select well-designed plastic containers or stylish glassware. I scour tag sales and flea markets for inspiring cups and glasses.

Photography by Sam Murphy

▶▶ MAKE YOUR OWN SILICONE ICE POP MOLDS

Time: **1–2 Hours (plus set time)** Complexity: **Moderate**

You can make incredibly imaginative pop molds with food-safe silicone rubber. Silicone picks up detail as faint as a fingerprint and is very flexible.

The process of making a silicone mold is easy. The liquid silicone is poured into a cup around an object, and then it hardens into a flexible mold. When the object is taken out of the mold, the negative space that it occupied makes a cavity for the pop mixture.

A silicone mold can be used over and over to create hundreds of ice pops. Molds can be made with multiple cavities, and several objects can be cast in the same mold, as long as there is a ⅜" space between them.

1. CHOOSE A PATTERN OBJECT

The original object shape that will be made into pops is called the master pattern. This pattern can be any shape, such as a small toy or other found object. Plastic or wood works best; glass and ceramic objects will stick to the silicone and are not practical for this purpose. You can also sculpt characters or shapes out of clay, wax, or wood to use as patterns. I use clay, which hardens so that I can easily pull it out of the silicone and use it again.

Most manufactured hard plastic ice pop molds are shaped with draft, which means they're angled slightly so you can pull the pops out easily. Consider draft when choosing your master pattern. The flexibility of silicone can accommodate small undercuts (grooves in the object), but master pattern objects that exhibit at least some draft are easiest to mold. The simplest objects to mold have a flat side, so they'll require only a 1-part mold. If there are holes or negative spaces in the pattern, fill them with clay so the liquid silicone won't seep in.

2. FIND OR MAKE A MOLD CONTAINER

You'll need a paper or plastic cup, or a yogurt or other food container ¼" to ⅜" larger than your master pattern on all sides. More than ⅜" of space around the object will only waste material and make the mold less flexible. If you can't find an existing container that's slightly bigger than your object, construct a box out of cardboard, sealing all seams with a hot glue gun so the container doesn't leak.

3. MAKE THE MOLD

Glue the flat side of the master pattern to the bottom of the container to keep the object from floating when you pour in the silicone. Draw a line on the container to indicate where the back of the object is positioned, because once the silicone is poured in, you won't be able to tell back from front. Later you may need to cut the mold in order to remove the object, and a cut will be less noticeable at the back.

To pre-measure the silicone, pour some uncooked rice into the container until there's a ⅜" layer of rice on top of the object. Pour the rice out into a measuring cup: this is the amount of silicone you'll need.

When you purchase the silicone, the package will have 2 bottles: the silicone and the catalyst. Thoroughly mix the silicone and catalyst together to make the amount you need; immediately they become activated and the slow hardening process begins.

Pour the mixed liquid silicone around the object until it covers it by ⅜". Tap the mold gently on a work surface to remove the air bubbles. (Alternatively, you can remove the bubbles by placing the mold on top of a running clothes dryer loaded with a few tennis balls for 30 minutes, or you can put it on top of a stereo speaker with the bass cranked up for 30 minutes and dance until the bubbles are gone.) Then let the silicone cure for 12–24 hours, or as directed on the package.

Mark a line on the hardened silicone that aligns with the line you drew on the container to indicate the back side of the object. Rip or cut the container away from the mold. Remove the master pattern; it might pop right out of the mold, but if you have trouble removing it, use a utility knife to cut a small slit in the backside of the mold to create an opening. Wash the mold with soap and water.

Photography by Ed Troxell

4. CAST THE ICE POPS

Close the slit (if you made one) with rubber bands or duct tape. Pour the pop mixture into the mold. Freeze for 20–30 minutes. When the mixture is partially frozen, insert the stick so it stands upright. It helps to surround the popsicle stick with other sticks perpendicularly to keep it in place. Freeze for 8 hours. Remove the rubber bands or tape, and remove the pop from the mold. Fabulous!

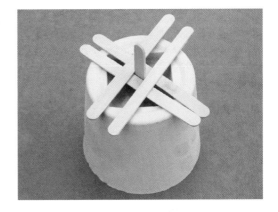

FINISH X

NOW GO USE IT »

▶▶ COOL DRAFTS

1. GOOD DRAFT
The pop will come out easily.

2. NO DRAFT
The pop will come out if it's allowed to melt slightly first.

3. BAD DRAFT
You will never get the pop out.

4. SMALL UNDERCUTS
The pop will come out with a little wiggling if the mold is made of flexible silicone.

5. LARGE UNDERCUTS
The pop will be very difficult to remove.

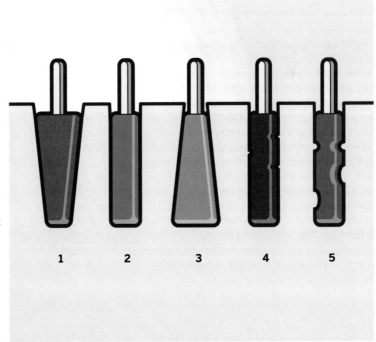

▶▶ MAKE MINI ICE POPS IN ICE CUBE TRAYS

1. MEASURE THE LID
Measure the outside rim of your ice cube tray and cut the lid material to the same size. Exact measurements will ensure a better grip when attaching binder clips.

2. CREATE A SPACER
Cut 7 strips of plastic or cardboard that will elevate the lid ⅜" above the tray: 2 that measure the length of the tray, and 5 that measure the distance between the 2 lengthwise strips. Glue the spacers around the rim of the tray, and glue 3 of them across the center to create additional supports.

3. DRAW A GRID FOR STICK PLACEMENT
Measure the center points of each ice cube cavity in your tray and the distance between the center points. Draw a grid on the lid to map out the center points.

4. MAKE SLOTS FOR THE STICKS
If you're using dowels for sticks, drill holes at the center points marked on the lid, using a drill bit the same width as the dowels. If you're using traditional pop sticks that are ⁷⁄₁₆" wide and ¹⁄₁₆" thick, cut slits to that size with a utility knife.

5. FILL THE POP TRAY AND FREEZE
Fill the tray no more than ¾ full with the pop mixture, because the ice will expand as it freezes. Use 2 binder clips on each short side of the tray and 3 binder clips on each long side of the tray to hold the lid on the tray. Insert the pop sticks or dowels and freeze for 3–4 hours.

6. REMOVE THE POPS AND ENJOY
Remove the binder clips and the lid. Let the pops sit at room temperature for 3–5 minutes before removing them from the mold.

MATERIALS

Ice cube tray(s)
Hot glue gun and glue sticks
1¼" binder clips (10 per tray)
¼" or ⅜" wooden dowels, or popsicle sticks
Utility knife
Drill and drill bit (optional) if you're using dowels

For a plastic lid:
⅛"- to ¼"-thick corrugated plastic, or ¹⁄₁₆"- to ⅛"-thick rigid plastic sheet
You can use styrene, PETG, or polypropylene.

For a cardboard lid:
⅛"- to ¼"-thick corrugated cardboard, or ⅛"-thick chipboard
Aluminum foil or plastic wrap to cover the cardboard

▶▶ INNOVATIVE ICE POPS

The recipes and techniques in *Pops! Icy Treats for Everyone* are a compilation of many years of testing flavors and shapes, experimenting with texture, and developing innovative freezing and mold-making techniques. My hope is that this book will encourage you to have fun creating pops that are uniquely your own. As a simple treat on a hot summer afternoon or an elegant finish to a special meal, ice pops can be as casual or fancy and as healthful or indulgent as you choose!

CARROT & WHEATGRASS POPS

INGREDIENTS
3½c apple juice
½c brown sugar
1½c peeled and diced carrots
1tsp ground ginger
½tsp cinnamon
1c coconut milk homemade or canned
1c wheatgrass juice freshly squeezed or prepared from tablets

Makes six 8oz pops or eight 6oz pops.

MATERIALS
Saucepan
Bowl
Food processor or blender
Ice pop molds

1. In a saucepan, combine the apple juice and brown sugar and stir over low heat for 5 minutes to dissolve the sugar. Set aside 1½c of the mixture.

2. To the remaining apple juice mixture in the saucepan, add the carrots, ginger, and cinnamon. Bring to a boil over high heat, then lower the heat and simmer for 15–20 minutes, until the carrots are soft. Remove from the heat and pour into a bowl to cool to room temperature.

3. In a food processor or blender, puree the carrot mixture until smooth. Add ½c of the coconut milk and process to combine.

4. In a bowl, combine the wheatgrass juice, ¾c of the reserved apple juice mixture, and the remaining ½c coconut milk.

5. Partially fill the ice pop molds with the carrot mixture. Insert the sticks. Freeze for at least 2 hours.

Add a layer of the wheatgrass mixture, freeze for 2 hours, then add a layer of the remaining reserved apple juice mixture, and repeat, freezing for at least 2 hours between layers, until the pop molds are full. Freeze for at least 4 hours.

6. Remove from the freezer; let stand at room temperature for 5 minutes before removing the pops from the molds. Replace your daily wheatgrass shot with one of the pops.

➕ See icypops.com for more recipes.

Photography by Emily Brooke Sandor

LOOKING GLASS

By Phil Daniel and Shawnee Langworthy

TRANSFORM A PLAIN WINDOW TO CREATE A ROOM WITH A VIBRANT VIEW.

➤➤ Originally created to decorate magnificent churches, stained glass windows have been around for at least 1,000 years. In modern times the materials and techniques for making stained glass have become much more accessible, making it a perfect hobby for those who enjoy designing and building.

Stained glass windows are perfect for adding a bit of privacy while still allowing some light to shine through. But much more than that, stained glass can transform a plain room into a place of stunning patterns and color.

With a simple design, even a beginner can create a stained glass window over just a weekend, and the results can provide pleasure for years to come.

» The Tiffany lamp, famous for its ornate stained glass shade, was created by stained glass designer Louis Comfort Tiffany in late 1895. The lamps were a way to use glass from leftover window pieces.

» Although churches and cathedrals were the first to use stained glass, today almost anything can be made into a stained glass mosaic, including the King himself, Elvis.

» Architect Frank Lloyd Wright also designed many of the stained glass panels for the houses he built, using his trademark patterns of geometric shapes.

Phil Daniel, a native of England, apprenticed in London and later in Minneapolis, where he started his own business in 1988. Phil Daniel Architectural Stained Glass combines the traditional aspects of custom-made stained glass with unique, contemporary vision. Shawnee Langworthy, a mosaic artist, has been working with Daniel since 2000.

Photography by Shawnee Langworthy; illustrations by Tim Lillis

WHAT YOU'LL NEED

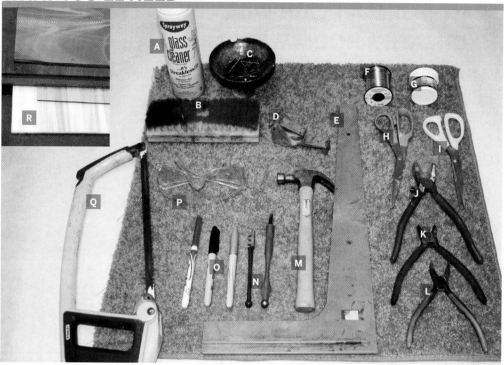

[A] Glass cleaner

[B] Bench brush

[C] Nails

[D] Lead vise

[E] Carpenter's square or straightedge

[F] 60/40 solder

[G] Flux

[H] Scissors

[I] Glass pattern scissors

[J] Running pliers (optional) These are helpful for breaking glass, but they're not necessary.

[K] Lead snips

[L] Grozing pliers

[M] Hammer

[N] Glass cutters

[O] Black Sharpie and marking pens

[P] Safety glasses

[Q] Hacksaw

[R] Glass variety of colors and textures

[NOT SHOWN]

Lead H came for leading the window. Lead strips for framing stained glass are called came. They come in H-section or U-section shapes.

Disposable gloves

Wood strips to create right angles

⅜" zinc border

Pencil

Paper as large as the window you're making

Kerosene or WD-40 to aid in cutting the glass

NOTE: Many of these items can be purchased through your local stained glass supply store, or online from stores like Glass Crafters (**glasscrafters.com**) and Delphi (**delphiglass.com**).

▶▶ GLORIFY YOUR WINDOWS WITH STAINED GLASS

Time: **A Weekend** Complexity: **Medium**

1. CREATE OR CHOOSE A DESIGN

Either create or find a simple design that will work for your window. I like to do geometric designs that emphasize the play of various glass contrasts with minimal color. Remember, with your first project the old saying "less is more" could be a good guiding principle.

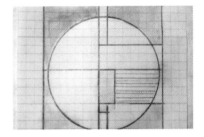

2. DRAW YOUR DESIGN

I decided to use a ⅜" zinc border, which is a nice standard size and supports a medium-sized window well. A larger window would need a wider border to accommodate it.

2a. With a pencil, draw the ⅜" border to scale on paper. With a black Sharpie, draw the inside lines of the design.

2b. Number the pieces of the design, then make 2 copies — 1 to cut out your pattern pieces and 1 for your layout.

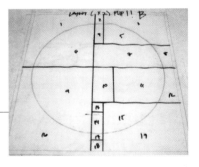

3. ADD A CUT LINE IN RED

Your outside pieces that get fit into the zinc border will require a cut line. To determine your cut line, lay the zinc on your layout. The cut line will be determined by the inside metal strip. The ⅜" zinc border shown has a ⅛" cut line. That means that ⅛" of the glass border pieces will slide into the zinc. We drew our cut line in red, ⅛" from the inside of our pencil border.

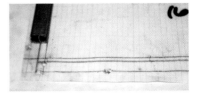

4. CUT OUT THE PATTERN PIECES

4a. Use your scissors to cut along the red cut line on one of your design copies.

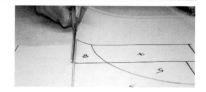

4b. Use your glass pattern shears to cut out the inside lines. Glass pattern shears have 3 blades, and they automatically remove the right amount of space that will be taken up by the leading between the glass pieces. Line up the middle of your Sharpie line with the middle of your scissors. Always cut in the same direction: if you begin cutting left to right, always cut left to right. If you start cutting out a circle clockwise, keep cutting in a clockwise direction. This ensures that your lines won't take little jogs to the right or left.

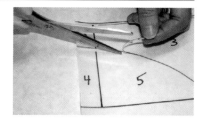

5. TRACE THE PATTERN PIECES ONTO GLASS

5a. Like putting a puzzle together, assemble your pattern pieces, using your layout copy as a guide.

5b. Put your pattern pieces on the glass you've chosen and trace them with a Sharpie or other glass-tracing permanent marker.

6. CUT OUT THE GLASS PIECES

6a. Dab the glass cutter in a little oil (kerosene is standard, but WD-40 works well). Start at 1 edge of the piece you're cutting. Apply a constant medium pressure while pushing the glass cutter's wheel along the inside of your Sharpie line until you get to the next edge. This is called scoring the glass. Always score from edge to edge. Perhaps practice on some scrap glass. After a few tries you'll get the feel for the right amount of pressure.

⚠️ CAUTION: Always wear safety glasses and make sure your glass cutter is sharp. Always clean the glass before cutting, and if the glass is textured, cut it on the smooth side. Also, you might feel more comfortable wearing gloves when breaking glass.

6b. Once your score is made, hold the glass with one thumb and forefinger on each side of the score, wrists away from the glass. Pull away and up with a snapping motion. If the score is good, the glass will snap right along your score line.

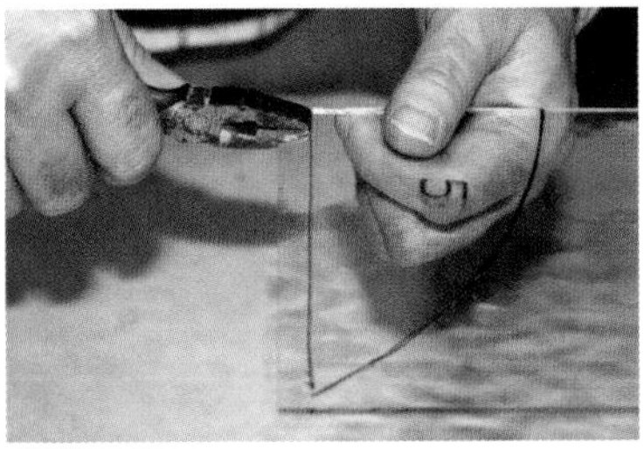

6c. Place your cut pieces onto your layout copy.

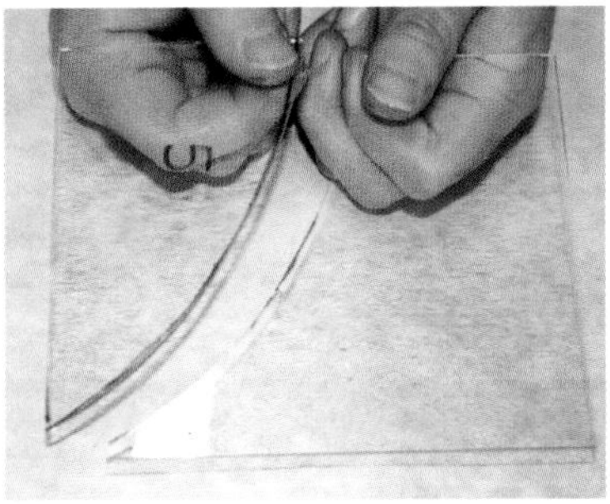

TIPS

» When cutting a straight line, you can slide the cutter along a straightedge.

» To break glass on a straight score line, use grozing pliers. With one hand, hold the pliers on one side of the score, flat jaw on top of the glass, curved jaw underneath. With the other hand, hold the glass on the opposite side of the score. Snap to break the glass along the score. It should snap off easily.

» If you're having trouble, use running pliers, which are made specifically for breaking glass along score lines.

7. CREATE A RIGHT ANGLE

Using a carpenter's square, align a few strips of wood to create a right angle to secure 1 corner of your window while you work. Nail the strips to your work surface so they come right up against the outside edge of where you have drawn your zinc border.

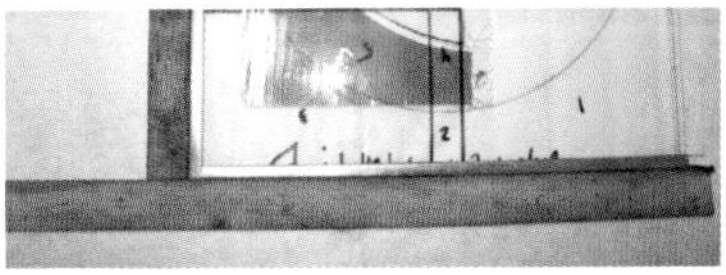

8. MARK AND CUT 2 ZINC BORDERS

8a. Lay a strip of zinc along the inside of the right angle where you've drawn the border. Mark its opposite edge. Cut the zinc to size with a hacksaw. Repeat to cut the second side of the zinc border, then fit it tightly into the right angle to meet the first.

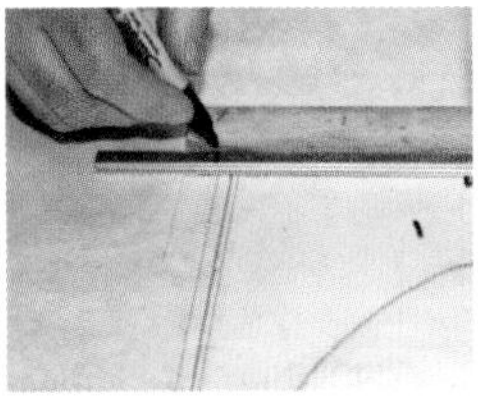

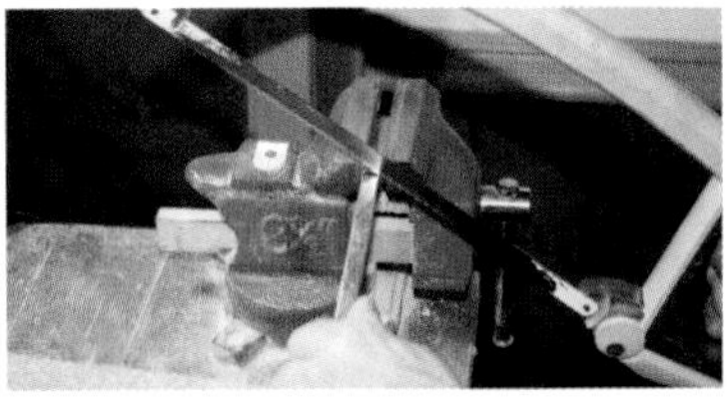

8b. Tack down the outside corners of the 2 zinc strips with nails, so they won't move around when you start leading.

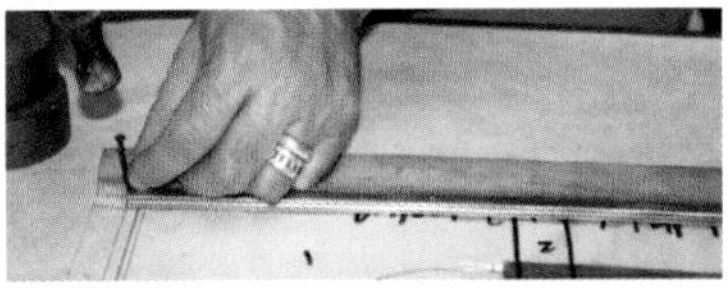

9. STRETCH THE LEAD H CAME

Lead strips for framing stained glass are called came. They come in H-section or U-section shapes. U came has 1 channel to hold glass and is used for border pieces. H came has 2 channels to hold glass, 1 on each side, and is used for the interior leading of a window.

The came is soft and should be stretched before use — if you don't stretch it, it may have kinks or undesirable bends in it. To stretch the H came, secure one end in the lead vise, then pull on the other end with grozing pliers.

⚠ CAUTION: Although metallic lead can't be absorbed through the skin, it can be absorbed through a cut, so I recommend wearing disposable gloves for protection.

10. LEAD THE WINDOW

10a. Place the corner piece of glass into the zinc border until it fits along your design lines. Measure and cut your first piece of lead came by holding it against the next exposed glass edge. Mark the lead about ⅛" in from the corners of the glass.

10b. Use the lead snips to cut the lead where marked. Hold the lead with the channel facing up, and the pliers at a right angle across the channel, and snip. Snipping the lead the wrong way will pinch the channel closed and you won't be able to slide the glass in. Once your measured strip of lead is cut, slide it onto the glass edge. Then fit the second piece of glass into the other channel of that H came.

10c. Hold the second piece of glass in place with a nail while you measure for the next piece of lead. Continue to cut and fit lead came and glass pieces until the window is completed to the outside edges.

Measure, cut, and fit the 2 remaining outside pieces of zinc border and tack them down with nails.

11. DAB FLUX ONTO THE LEAD AND ZINC JOINTS

Flux allows the solder to stick to the lead and zinc. Wherever the ends of the lead came or zinc come together, use a brush to dab the joint with a liberal amount of flux. Flux generously; you can clean off the excess later.

12. SOLDER THE WINDOW

12a. Plug in your soldering iron. It should be hot enough to melt the solder, but not the lead came. You can test this with some lead scraps. Hold the solder above the area you want to join. Gently lay the flat end of the soldering iron tip on top of the solder and move in a slight circular motion.

12b. As the solder melts, pull the iron away and the solder should bead nicely above the joint. The key is to work it as little and as gently as possible, and to flux it well anywhere you want solder to be. You can always use the iron to smooth out a larger blob of solder and use the corners of the iron to tap it into a corner. Be careful, however, to avoid hitting the glass with the iron and breaking it.

12c. Continue to solder all the joints where lead and/or zinc meet. Don't remove the nails that hold the window together until you've soldered all the joints between the lead and the zinc frame. Once one whole side is soldered, remove the remaining flux with a cloth, flip the panel over, then flux and solder the other side.

13. CLEAN THE WINDOW AND BURNISH THE LEAD

Remove the remaining marker, flux, and residue with glass cleaner and a cotton cloth. You can also buy a cement mixture at stained glass supply stores that can be used to fill in any spaces between the glass and lead. If you choose to cement your window, this mixture will also clean the glass and burnish the lead.

To give the lead an aged look, burnish it with a bench brush. Light, rapid brushing of the lead and solder joints will make them fade to a darker gray and look less shiny. Enjoy your beautiful stained glass window!

FINISH ☒

FAUX STAINED GLASS

▶▶ CRAFT A QUICK AND EASY
WINDOW COVER. By Mark Montano

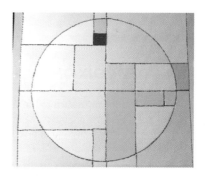

MATERIALS

Transparent plastic folders in different colors. Most office supply or dollar stores carry them.
Hot glue gun with silver glue sticks
Tape, scissors, and thick black marker
Large sheet of paper on which to draw your design

Time: **1 Hour** Complexity: **Easy**

I certainly appreciate the craftsmanship of stained glass, but I've come up with something that gives a similar effect without the prerequisite labor. Though it may not look exactly like stained glass, it's a quick and easy rendition that easily jazzes up my windows.

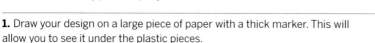

1. Draw your design on a large piece of paper with a thick marker. This will allow you to see it under the plastic pieces.

2. Decide which colors go where, then lay your plastic folders over your drawing and start tracing the shapes. Use 2 colors together to create different colors, such as blue and red to make purple, just as with paint.

3. Cut out your shapes and place them on your drawing.

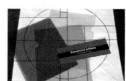

4. Once all the pieces are cut out and placed on the design, tape them together with very small pieces of tape. Fold over the end of the tape so it's easy to remove while you work.

5. Using your hot glue gun, glue your pieces together along the seams where they meet. Wipe off the tip of the glue gun regularly with an old rag to keep your beads of glue neat.

6. Glue all around the edges of your stained glass piece to give it a finished edge.

7. Using small pieces of tape, place the faux stained glass on your window to position it where you want it.

8. Using tiny beads of clear hot glue, adhere the stained glass piece to your window every 5" or so. You can easily remove it when it's time for a change.

Mark Montano is the author of five books, including *The Big-Ass Book of Crafts*. He can be seen regularly as the host of TLC's *10 Years Younger* and as a designer on *While You Were Out*.

Photography by Auxy Espinoza

Photography courtesy of Nancy Micholson, Phil Daniel, Visions Gallery, and Vit-Mar Stained Glass Studio

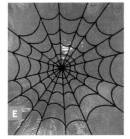

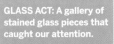

GLASS ACT: A gallery of stained glass pieces that caught our attention.

A, F, and I: Streetscapes brought to life. nancy-nicholson.com

B and C: Free stained glass patterns from stainedglass.on.ca.

D, G, and H: These evoke Frank Lloyd Wright's classics. phildaniel.com

E: Among Carolyn Insler's numerous stained glass pieces is this fetching spider web. visionsgallery.com

SWING
SHIFT

By Christine Haynes

RUFFLE UP A SUMMER CLASSIC OR KEEP IT SIMPLE.

▶▶ This project is like learning to make a whole closet full of skirts and dresses. Follow the steps and you'll have a simple dress or skirt that is endlessly alterable.

For the dress, you can make it as a halter, with shoulder ties, with straps, or strapless.

The skirt is made with a simple elastic waistband, but is brought up a notch with the addition of circular ruffles, which are incredibly easy to make in the length of your choice. Make them long for a full flounce, or make them short and sweet — it's completely up to you. And once you learn how easy it is to make ruffles, you'll be putting them everywhere.

» The English word *halter* comes from the German word for "holder," as in *Büstenhalter*.

» In 1955, French fashion designer Christian Dior coined the term *A-line* to describe the funnel-like silhouette for his new collection.

» Spanish flamenco dancers are famous for wearing long dresses with layers of ruffles.

Christine Haynes is an independent fashion designer based in Los Angeles. Her first book, *Hip to Hem: Simple-to-Sew Clothes for Every Season* will be published by Potter Craft in April 2009. To learn more about Christine or her upcoming book, visit her website at christinehaynes.com.

Photograph by Jen Siska; illustrations by Tim Lillis

WHAT YOU'LL NEED

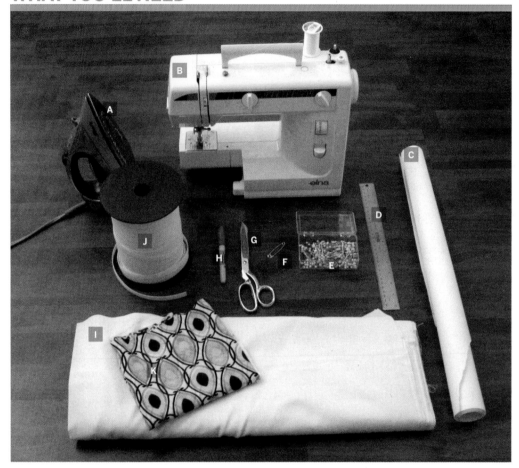

[A] Iron

[B] Sewing machine

[C] Paper roll

[D] Ruler or T square

[E] Straight pins

[F] Large safety pin

[G] Scissors

[H] Marker

[I] Muslin

[J] ½" elastic
amount depends on your
sizing in Step 4

[K] Fabric of your choice
amount depends on your
sizing in Step 2

⏩ FILL YOUR WARDROBE WITH FLOUNCES AND FRILLS BY ADDING TO THIS SIMPLE SHIFT

Time: **2–10 Hours** Complexity: **Easy to Medium**

1. MAKE THE RUFFLE PATTERN

1a. To make a circle pattern (donut-shaped) for the ruffle, determine how long you'd like your ruffles to hang. To make the ruffles the same size as I have, use the following measurements. For the large ruffles on the dress: 25" diameter with a 7"-diameter center circle. For the small ruffles on the skirt: 10" diameter with a 3½"-diameter center circle.

1b. Using either muslin or paper to create your ruffle pattern, make a mark for the center of the circle. Measure out from this center point to where you want the outer circle to be, and mark dots in equal distance from this center point. Connect these dots to make a circle.

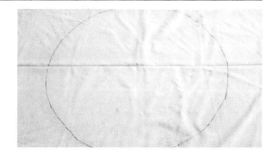

1c. Marking from the same center point, measure the distance for a center circle. Again, mark dots in equal distance from the center point and then connect the dots to make the center circle.

1d. Using a ruler, make a straight line to connect the small center circle to the outside larger circle. Now you should have what looks like a donut with a line on one side.

1e. Following the line you just drew, cut along to the center circle. Next, cut along the outside circle, then around the small center circle. Now you have a circle ruffle pattern.

Pin the pattern to your fabric and cut around the outside of the large circle, then cut the center circle and the line that connects the 2. Open the ruffle so that the center circle becomes a straight line, and you'll see how the center circle becomes the top of the ruffle, and the rest flows down to make the flounce.

2. MAKE THE DRESS/SKIRT PATTERN

The basis for both the skirt and dress is a simple A-line shift dress. It isn't fitted, so sizing is quite easy. The versions I've made for the project are for a size small. Use the measurements at right to make your dress or skirt look like these.
NOTE: **These measurements are for ½ of the dress or skirt. You'll be making 2 pieces and sewing them together at the side seams.**

Size	Top width	Bottom width	Length
Extra Small	23"	35"	25"
Small	25"	36"	26"
Medium	27"	38"	27"
Large	29"	40"	28"

2a. To make the pattern, measure out the top width using a ruler and marker. Find the center point of the top width. From that point, measure and mark down the length of your choice. Do the same from each end point of the top width. You should now have what looks like a big E.

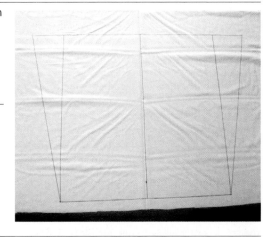

2b. Take your bottom width and cut the number in half. Measure and mark that half measurement on either side of the center point along the bottom width. Using a ruler, connect the corners of the top width to the bottom width.

2c. Cut out the dress and skirt pattern by cutting around the outside lines. This is ½ of your dress or skirt. The front and back of the dress/skirt are mirror images, so to cut out the pieces, place the pattern on your fabric and cut it out twice. You can fold your pattern in half and place it on the fold of your fabric to save cutting.

3. SEW THE DRESS/SKIRT WITH RUFFLES

3a. Using a zigzag stitch, finish off all raw edges of the cut fabric you'll be using. Then line up your 2 pieces, right sides facing, and stitch the side seams together using a straight stitch and a ⅝" seam allowance.

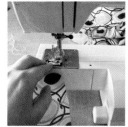 

3b. It may take multiple ruffle circles joined at the short ends to go around your garment. Eyeball how many it might take, and connect them on the ends with right sides facing. For my examples, I used 5 ruffles on the dress at its widest point, and 7 ruffles on the skirt at its widest point. Once you have as many joined as needed, with the wrong side of the ruffle facing the right side of the dress or skirt, line up the top of your ruffle with the top edge of the dress or skirt and pin in place.

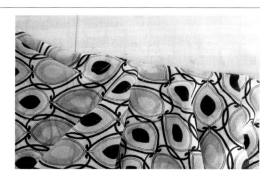

3c. When you go around the whole top and the 2 short ends meet, you might have some ruffle left over. If so, fold back 1 side and trim, leaving yourself the ⅝" seam allowance to attach the 2 ends together. Stitch the 2 short ends together, right sides facing, and pin to the dress.

3d. Stitch the ruffle to the top of the dress with a straight stitch. Press up the hem of the ruffle and stitch in place with a straight stitch. Flip up the ruffle and measure from the seam down to where you'd like to sew the next ruffle. There are no rules on how close or far it needs to be. This is all up to you and will depend on how long your ruffles are. For the dress, I placed the ruffles 6" below, so there would be 3" overlapping. Pin the ruffle to the dress, and repeat Steps 3b and 3c to attach and finish the next ruffle.

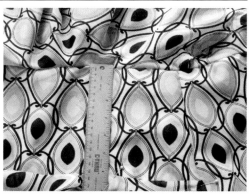

3e. Repeat Step 3d for each additional ruffle, until you've attached as many as you'd like.

3f. Press up the hem of the dress or skirt and stitch in place with a straight stitch. Fold the top of the dress or skirt down 1½", including the ruffle, into the inside of the garment, and press. Lifting the ruffle out of the way, pin the fold down to the inside of the garment. Starting at 1 side seam, stitch around the bottom of the fold with a straight stitch, leaving a 1" opening from where you started.

NOTE: Be very careful not to sew the ruffle while doing this.

4. ADD ELASTIC

4a. Cut the ½" elastic to fit either your bust or your waist, depending on whether you're making a skirt or a dress. For this garment, I recommend using the measurements at right as a guide.

	Extra Small	Small	Medium	Large
Dress	27"	28"	29"	30"
Skirt	25"	26"	27"	28"

4b. Attach a large safety pin to 1 end of your elastic and feed it through the 1" hole you left in the casing.

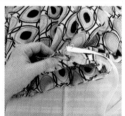

4c. Push the elastic around the entire garment. Be careful not to twist the elastic or lose the other end in the casing. Pull the elastic out, and pin to the other end, overlapping about 1". Sew the 2 ends together using a zigzag stitch, then fit the elastic into the casing. Close up the hole with a straight stitch.

4d. To wear, flip the top with the elastic to the inside of the dress or skirt, so the ruffle appears to come out from the inside seamlessly. Adjust the gathering on the ruffles, and you're done!

FINISH

SEWING THE DRESS OR SKIRT WITHOUT RUFFLES

Love the shape, but not the ruffles? Well, you certainly don't have to add them if you don't want to! To make your version without the ruffles:

1. Follow all of Step 2.
2. Follow Step 3a.
3. Press up the hem of the dress or skirt and stitch in place with a straight stitch.
4. Fold the top of the dress or skirt down 1½", into the inside of the garment and press. Pin the fold down to the inside of the garment. Starting at 1 side seam, stitch around the bottom of the fold with a straight stitch, leaving a 1" opening from where you started.
5. Follow all of Step 4.

 ## OPTIONAL STRAPS OR BELT

Not into the strapless look? Or maybe you'd like to make a belt like I did with the black dress? Well, here's how! Oh, and don't forget, you can use any fabric you'd like: contrasting, matching, or whatever!

Making a Belt

Decide how long and wide you'd like your belt to be. For the black dress I made it 60" long and 1½" wide. Cut a piece of fabric the length of your choice by the width of your choice doubled, plus a ⅝" seam allowance. If my belt is 60" long by 1½" wide, my fabric is 60"×3⅝". Fold the piece in half, lengthwise, right sides facing, and sew along the long end with a ⅝" seam allowance. Turn it right side out and press. I left the ends unfinished and tied them into knots to match the shoulder ties. But if you'd like them finished, turn the ends into the inside of the belt, press, and straight-stitch closed. Re-press.

Making Shoulder Ties

To make shoulder ties like on the black dress, follow the instructions for making a belt, but make it long enough to total the 4 straps. For the black dress, I made each strap 20" long, so I cut my piece 80"×3⅝". Once you've turned your piece right side out and pressed it, cut it into four 20" pieces. Pin 1 end into the inside of your dress, lining up the bottom of the strap with the bottom of the casing. Straight-stitch the strap in place along the same stitching used for the casing. Stitch the strap again, on top of the casing, just above the

elastic. Be careful not to catch the elastic. Repeat with the other 3 straps. Either tie the ends into knots or finish them off per the directions in the belt section.

Making a Halter

Follow the instructions for making a belt, but make 2 pieces, approximately 30"×3⅝". For a halter, it's best to place the 2 ties at a slight angle, toward your neck, so the straps don't buckle. Pin the 2 pieces inside your dress and sew in place, but try it on just before sewing to make sure the ties are placed properly. Tie the straps behind your neck.

Making Straps

If you want simple straps, follow the instructions for the shoulder ties, but make only 2 straps. Sew them the same way as the shoulder ties.

Photograph by Jen Siska

Travel Crafty

PORTLAND

The city boasts destinations galore to keep visitors busy.

Portland has a reputation as a crafty city, and with good reason. If you're planning a visit, check out the frequent craft fairs, classes and workshops, and the world-class Museum of Contemporary Craft. But for great shopping, these four destinations are dear to my heart.

YARNIA

4183 S.E. Division St. yarniapdx.com

"Come, let's make yarn," says the Yarnia website. Indeed, this is a store where the shelves are lined with big cones of single-filament fibers: wool, cotton, silk, mohair, acrylic — you name it. You select just the fibers and colors you want, and Yarnia's staff will wind you a cone of your own custom yarn, right on the spot.

Owner Lindsey Ross (pictured at top left), herself an avid knitter, will help you figure out how much yarn you'll need, and what fibers will combine best for your project. It's enough to make you weep, really.

Get a healthy vegetarian lunch at Kalga Cafe, just up the street at 4147 S.E. Division. They serve Mexican, Middle Eastern, and Thai food, and they make a yummy vegan pizza.

Diane Gilleland runs DIY Alert (diyalert. com), a website devoted to all things crafty in Portland, Ore.

Photography by Virginia Meyers

COOL COTTONS
2417 S.E. Hawthorne Blvd. coolcottonsinc.com

As the name implies, Cool Cottons has bolts and bolts of high-quality cotton prints and canvas, suitable for quilts, skirts, bags, and home decor. The store is spread out in an old house, so you wander from room to room, discovering pretty colors and patterns.

Co-owners Pam Oakes and Marie Ritten are passionate about fabric, and it's contagious. You'll often find them piling bolts on the shop's worktable, helping a customer find just the right print for a project.

Hike across the street to Grand Central Baking Company for one of their famous Triple Chocolate Cookies. grandcentralbakery.com

KNITTN' KITTEN
7530 N.E. Glisan St. knittnkitten.com

"The Kitten," as it's affectionately known by locals, is a craft supply thrift store. Rome Church combs estate sales and flea markets for craft materials, and then stocks this little shop she co-owns with her mother, Ethel Stark, with her best finds. On any visit to Knittn' Kitten, you're likely to find treasure in the form of vintage fabrics, miles of rickrack, notions, beads, buttons, stitchery supplies, vintage patterns, and more.

The prices are incredibly reasonable — real, thrift-store reasonable. Every person I've taken to the Knittn' Kitten has left with a big bag of goodies and a huge smile on her face.

Recharge from your craft-thrifting spree with a cup of coffee and a scone across the street at Spill the Bean Coffee Shop, 7631 N.E. Glisan.

TWISTED
2310 N.E. Broadway twistedpdx.com

Twisted has the feel of a crafty person's living room. Shannon Squire and Emily Kizer, who co-own Twisted, make everyone who steps through the door feel welcomed. There are cozy couches and chairs for knitting with your friends, and a lovely selection of loose-leaf teas to sip. And to distract you from relaxing, there are craft supplies.

Twisted specializes in sock yarn — there's an entire wall of it here. You can also find yarns for your garment projects, supplies for needle felting, and embroidery flosses and tools. It can be overwhelming, so perhaps you'd better curl up on one of those comfy chairs with some tea.

Snack on the Gourmet Cheese Plate and some homemade soup at Costello's, just down the street at 2222 N.E. Broadway. costellostravelcaffe.com

 # MAPPED OUT

Build a Google map of your town's hot spots.
By Diane Gilleland

If your city is craft-friendly, create a useful Crafty Google Map. Crafters from all over will thank you!

1. GET A GOOGLE ACCOUNT.
If you use other Google products, like Gmail or Google Reader, then you already have one. If not, set one up for free at google.com/accounts.

2. MAKE A BIG LIST.
Decide what locations (galleries, shops, cafés, etc.) you want to include on your map. You can cover the whole city, or just a handful of your favorite haunts. You'll need the street address of each place.

✳ **TIP: If you're going for all-inclusive, try doing a search in Google Maps for terms like "craft supplies" and "art supplies" in your city.**

3. START YOUR MAP.
Go to maps.google.com. Click on the My Maps tab, then click Create a New Map. From there, add a name and a description to your map.

4. ADD A PLACEMARK.
In the search bar at the top of the Google Maps page, enter the address of a location you want to include on your map. Click the Search Maps button. This location will appear on your map as a place-mark. Look in the placemark information box for the Save to My Maps link. Click it, and select your map from the menu. If you live in a city that has Google Street View, you'll see a photo of the place.

5. CUSTOMIZE YOUR PLACEMARK.
Click on your new placemark and bring up its infor-mation window to add your own info. You could add things like store hours, phone numbers, or what kinds of supplies they carry. Look at the information window to find a Rich Text Editor. Use this to add bold, italic, or colored text, or to build a hyperlink. When you've added all the material you want to the placemark, click the OK button.

6. DOUBLE-CHECK THE LOCATION!
Google warns us: "Landmark placements are approximate." So when Google Maps finds a loca-tion, double-check it. Find the menu at the top of your map and click Satellite. Use the slider at the top to zoom in. At maximum zoom there's an aerial image that will usually confirm whether your placemark is in the right place. I found that Google located Collage (my favorite shop) a few doors down from where it actually is. This is easily fixed — simply drag the placemark to the correct location.

7. CONSIDER COLOR-CODING.
If you have many locations, you can color-code your placemarks. Click on the large blue pin symbol in the placemark information window and find a menu of colors and symbols. In my Portland map, I use blue for craft supply stores, green for craft schools, yellow for thrift stores, and purple for boutiques.

8. ADD ZONES.
If your town has specific neighborhoods that are noteworthy, you can use Google Maps' shape tool to draw a zone marker on your map. Click on the Shape button at the top left corner of your map. Then draw a rectangle (or whatever shape you like) around an area by clicking on each point of the shape. You can then add notes about this zone.

9. CONSIDER COLLABORATING.
If it's too much to build a Crafty Google Map by yourself, you can collaborate with a few friends. (Each will need to have a Google account.) Click on the Collaborate link and follow the directions.

10. PLACE YOUR MAP ON A WEBSITE.
To show off your Google map, click on Link to This. Then copy and paste the HTML code into your own website or blog.

➕ For Diane's Google map of Portland, go to diyalert.com/crafty_portland_map.

Rustic Wood Side Table

Just the right branch and a slice of trunk make this simple sidekick. BY JOE SZUECS

Photograph by Sam Murphy

I had a dying madrone (*Arbutus menziesii*) in my backyard. Looking at its structure, I noticed a nice 3-pronged junction of branches a few feet above my head. I thought this would make a nice tripod base for a small side table, so with a bit of trial and error and a slice of another tree trunk for the top, this little rustic side table was born.

The antithesis to mass-produced commercial goods, this piece is funky and original by definition, made with found forest objects. It comes with a guarantee that no one else will have one just like it.

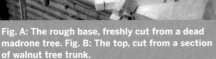

Fig. A: The rough base, freshly cut from a dead madrone tree. Fig. B: The top, cut from a section of walnut tree trunk.

Fig. C: Evening out the top with a belt sander. Note the wood blocks used to secure it. Fig. D: Fine sanding with an orbital sander makes the top silky smooth.

Materials

» Tripod-like tree branch
» Cross-section of tree trunk
» Saw
» Various sanding devices
» Dowel screw
» Drill and bits
» Vise-Grips or other locking pliers

1. Find a suitable branch junction.

For the base of your table, you'll need to find a tree branch like mine. The branches should be thick enough, about 1½", to support a reasonable load: at least a stack of books or magazines, although probably not a person (Figure A).

It's unlikely that you'll have a suitable tree on your, your landlord's, or your neighbor's property. Check with a local arborist. They cut down trees all day long. Let them know what you're up to, and for little or no money they'll probably have a nice base for you in a few days.

✳ TIPS: Look for a deciduous hardwood. Conifers won't offer 3- or 4-branched junctions. They're also filled with sticky gummy resin. It's also best to find a tree that's been dead for a while. The wood will be dry and stable, which is preferable.

If you do have a tree available, grab a saw and cut it down. Now, downing trees is pretty dangerous work. My tree was small and manageable. If you don't have much experience with tree work, find someone with experience to help.

When obtaining your base, leave plenty of extra length on all the legs.

2. Get a slice of trunk for the top.

For the top of the table, you'll want a cross-section of a larger tree, about 10" to 12" in diameter. Once again, an arborist is your best bet. Just have them cut a few cross-sections of a tree trunk. Ask them to cut 2" to 3" slabs and to make them as even as possible (Figure B). In this case, it will be difficult to find dry wood. So just go with "green" hardwood. I recommend maple, oak, or walnut.

Photography by Joe Szuecs

Fig. E: The dowel screw that will connect the top to the base. Fig. F: The dowel screw in place in the underside of the tabletop. Fig. G: Marking the base for trimming. Choose the perfect height for your aesthetics.

Fig. H: The base, stripped of bark, and the top, ready for attachment. Fig. I: A hole drilled in the top of the base for the dowel screw.

NOTE: Depending on the type of tree and time of year, the bark may or may not peel easily. For this project, I peeled the bark off the base and left it on the top. Any way works, so it's up to you.

Before you move on with the project, inspect your base and top for any signs of insect damage or rot. Numerous neat holes in the surface of the wood are indicative of insect infestation. So are fine dust or granules. If either of these conditions exist, go back to Step 1. You don't want to inadvertently introduce wood-eating beasties into your home.

Finally, it's highly likely that the cross-section for your top will form, or already has, radiating cracks. The outer rings of the cross-section are less dense than the center rings. As the wood dries, the amount of shrinkage is greater in the less dense areas. This is normal and, in my opinion, adds character.

As an alternative to rough wood, some Asian restaurant supply stores offer cutting boards that are simply sections of tree trunks. One of these will make a fine top for the side table.

You can find some at wokshop.com, in with the cleavers and knives.

3. Tame the top.

Take a look at your trunk cross-section. One side is going to be easier to work, having fewer deep saw marks, for example, than the other. You'll save yourself some work by making that the top surface.

A belt sander will make evening out the top surface a breeze. Start with a rough grit, like 50. Now, just grind that sucker flat.

You'll notice in Figure C that I screwed 2 pieces of scrap wood into my worktable to secure the cross-section while sanding. Unless you like stopping fast-moving chunks of wood with a tender area of your body, this technique is highly recommended.

Remember to rotate the top occasionally to even out the grit marks. If you don't have access to a belt sander, use an orbital sander with 60-grit paper. It will take longer and you'll use more sandpaper.

Turn the top over and clean up the bottom. You don't need to be perfect here, just even it out a bit.

Change the belt to a medium grit, 100 or 120. Work the top surface until smooth. Finally, using an orbital sander and 120- or 150-grit paper, sand the top surface even smoother (Figure D).

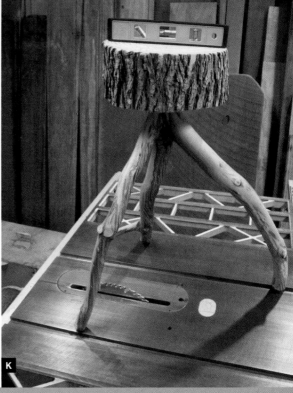

Fig. J: The base and underside of the top are attached together with the dowel screw. Make sure to tighten securely.

Fig. K: Use a level to make sure your creation doesn't tilt to one side. Don't assume that your floor is true.

4. Join the top to the bottom.

Connecting the tabletop to the base is easy. In most hardware stores you'll find something called a dowel screw: basically, 2 screws connected head to head (Figure E). Select the largest dowel screw that fits; it shouldn't be longer than the top is thick.

Select a drill bit that's almost as wide in diameter as the dowel screw. Just line them up and eyeball it. You want the screw threads about ⅛" to ¼" wider than the bit. Make a mark in the center of the bottom (underside) of the top. Drill a hole as deep as ½ the length of the dowel screw. Be very careful not to drill through the top (Figure F).

✳ **TIP: Wrap a small piece of tape around the drill bit at the desired depth before you drill.**

Trim the stem of the base to a length that suits you. Cut parallel to the limb joint (Figures G and H).

Drill a hole directly in the middle of the base stem (Figure I). If you taped your bit, drill to that depth. Using Vise-Grips or other pliers, screw the dowel screw into the top. It should penetrate to the middle of the screw. Now, using the top for torque, screw the stem to the base (Figure J). Tighten it well.

5. Level.

Set the table on its legs. Check the level with, well, a level (Figure K). It helps to check the level of the surface your project is sitting on as well. Don't assume that your floor is true.

Trim the legs down to about the height you desire, but a little longer. Using the level and a saw, trim the bottoms of the legs until you get the tabletop perfectly level. This sounds simpler than it may actually be to accomplish.

6. Finish.

If your top was pretty green, you should wait to apply a finish. How long? Weeks. Months. You can use mineral oil or walnut oil to provide some protection while it's drying.

Once it's dry, sand the top with 220- or 240-grit sandpaper. If you don't like the cracks in the top, fill them with an appropriately hued wood filler and re-sand. Apply any wood finish you like. If you oiled it, you want to avoid water-based finishes.

Joe Szuecs, pronounced *sooch*, lives in western Sonoma County, Calif., and owns Renga Arts (renga-arts.com), a store that sells products made from recycled and reclaimed materials.

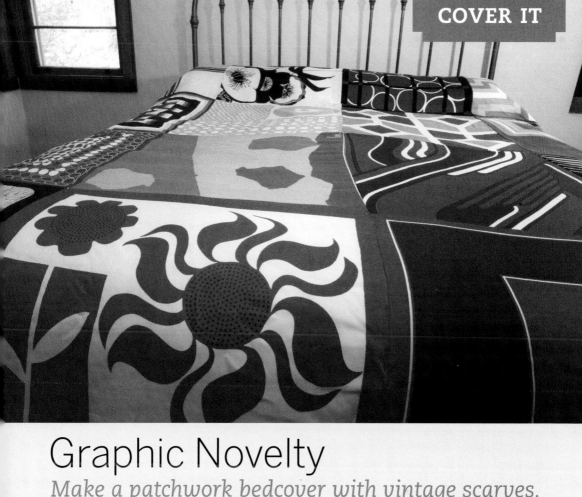

Graphic Novelty

Make a patchwork bedcover with vintage scarves.

BY LINDSAY BROWN AND SARAH GEE

W e love the abstract geometric shapes found on women's scarves from the 1960s and 70s. With their bright colors and bold motifs, each scarf is like a modern abstract painting.

As vintage fabric collectors, we've amassed a large collection of scarves that we were unable to use in the making of our other home decor products. Since the bold graphic effect of these scarves is mostly lost when wrapped around the body, we decided to find a way to put them on display. A bedspread seemed the ideal way to exhibit their full potential.

Fig. A: Lay out your scarves to find a nice composition. We rejected a few of these scarves in favor of ones we preferred. **Fig. B:** Use sharp scissors to cut your scarves. They should all be identical in size. **Fig. C:** With right sides together, serge each scarf to the next using a 4-thread serging hem or the method of your choice. **Fig. D:** Once you have 4 strips of 4 scarves each, serge them together to make the silk side of your bedcover.

Materials

- » **16 vintage scarves** approximately 26"–27" square, made of silk, rayon, acetate, or similar fabric
- » **5yds hemp/cotton fabric** medium-weight for backing, in a light color with subtle or no pattern
- » **3–4 cones of serger thread** in light gray or pale sage green, for scarf side
- » **1 spool of polyester or cotton thread** in a neutral color, for backing
- » **Serger and pins**
- » **Large, very sharp sewing scissors**
- » **Chalk or permanent marker**
- » **Double-sided tape for sewing**
- » **25½" square of corrugated cardboard** to cut a template

1. Collect scarves.

Although you'll use 16 scarves arranged in a 4×4 grid, collect a few more to ensure a set that matches.

The scarves should be 26" or 27" square to make a bedcover approximately 100" square, which will fit a queen or king mattress.

2. Design your bedcover.

Lay out your scarves — there are no rules (Figure A). Play around with your composition until it clicks.

3. Cut the template and scarves.

Cut every scarf to the exact dimensions you decide upon (Figure B). For our 4×4 scarf bedspread, we use a template of exactly 25½" square, which works well with most scarves. Cut your scarves any smaller and you'll start to lose the scarf's design.

Make a 25½" square template out of cardboard, and use a fine permanent marker or chalk line marker to rule lines on the scarves before you cut. Use a light pressure with your drawing tool: scarves, even silk, are stretchy and they don't keep still!

4. Sew the scarves together.

Make 4 strips of 4 scarves each, using 3- or 4-thread serging. Serge one scarf to the next (Figure C) until you have a strip of 4. Make 3 more strips (Figure D), then serge your 4 strips together. You should now

Photography by Lindsay Brown

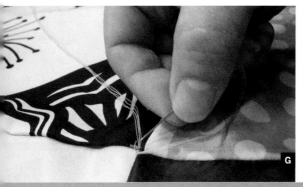

Fig E: The reversible bedspread should have a medium-weight backing in a neutral color. Fig. F: Place the silk side and the backing right sides together and pin them around the edges.

Fig. G: Tack the silk side to the backing, at all 9 points in the grid. Fig. H: The Vintage Scarf Bedspread is fully reversible!

have a flowy bedspread approximately 100" square. Iron it on medium-low heat.

✳ **TIP: Since silk or polyester is slippery, it's hard to keep the 2 starting edges lined up exactly. To solve this, join right sides together with double-sided tape before serging.**

5. Make the backing.
We used an organic hemp/cotton medium-weight fabric for the backing. Since many scarves are semi-translucent, your fabric should be relatively light in color. Pre-shrink it before cutting.

Our fabric comes in 60" widths, so to make a 100" square backing, we cut 3 pieces: 60"×101", 41"×60", and 41"×41" (Figure E). Serge or sew, with a straight stitch, the 2 short pieces together. Then serge this strip to the long piece. You now have a backing with 2 perpendicular seams. Iron it.

6. Measure and trim the silk side.
Your scarf piece should be somewhere between 99" and 101" square depending on your seam allowances and serging style. It may be a little uneven in places, so trim it accordingly until it's adequately

square. Now measure and trim the hemp backing to match the silk side exactly.

7. Sew the silk side to the backing.
Place the silk side and the backing right sides together and pin them around the edges (Figure F). Starting at a corner, serge the entire edge together except the last 8"–10". Carefully pull the whole thing inside out through the opening. Then topstitch around the entire edge of the bedcover, ¼" from the edge.

8. Tack the backing to the scarves.
The silk side can become billowy, so we tack it to the backing with a single stitch at every point in the grid, 9 in all (Figure G). Tie off your ends discreetly.

➕ For washing instructions, go to craftzine.com/08/cover_bedcover.

Lindsay Brown and Sarah Gee are designers from Vancouver, British Columbia, Canada. ounodesign.com

Simple Bauhaus Throw

Knit a blanket inspired by the clean lines of this early modernist art movement. BY LISA SHOBHANA MASON

O n any given Saturday, you might find me strolling around a museum or gallery. I enjoy viewing artists' unique interpretations of universal themes and elements, and I'm drawn to the repetition of various designs throughout the ages. From the bold, outsider art vibe of the Gee's Bend quilts to the vivacious designs of the late 1960s, great artworks and movements influence and inspire many of my pieces.

When I designed this blanket, I was thinking of the Bauhaus art movement with its stern and unadorned style. My aim was to create a piece that is sleek and clean, as well as moody and sumptuous. This throw adds warmth to an ultramodern decor, giving the Bauhaus Geometric Throw a 21st-century look.

Photography by Brian Steege

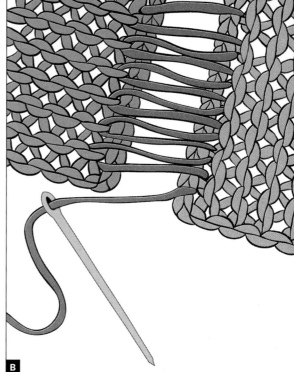

Fig A: This knitted throw has four 26"×26" squares, making the entire blanket 52"×52". The direction of garter ridges alternates between horizontal and vertical for added interest.

Fig: B: The 4 knitted squares are joined together with a mattress stitch. Each square is turned 90° before it's attached so that the garter ridge runs in a different direction.

Materials

» 2 skeins of Lorna's Laces Heaven yarn, 90% mohair, 10% nylon, 975yds (891m), 7oz (198g), 1 each in colors Pewter (A) and Blackberry (B) or substitute 975yds (891m) of any worsted-weight mohair yarn for each color.

» U.S. size 10 (6mm) circular knitting needle, 29"–32" (74cm–80cm) long If necessary, change the needle size to obtain the correct gauge.

» Tapestry needle
Gauge: 14 stitches and 28 rows = 4" (10cm) in garter stitch.

CONSTRUCTION NOTES

This throw has four 26"×26" squares, for a total size of 52"×52", arranged so that one color shows horizontal garter ridges and the other vertical ridges.

Illustration by Alison Kendall

EXCERPTED FROM *YARNPLAY* (NORTH LIGHT BOOKS), BY LISA SHOBHANA MASON.

Mason demonstrates how to mix yarns, colors, and textures to create graphic hand-knit pieces, including sweaters, tanks, hats, scarves, blankets, washcloths, and more. And for free-thinkers, Mason teaches how to take a pattern and make it your own.

1. Knit.

Cast on 92 stitches. Work in garter stitch until the square measures 26". Bind off.

Knit 2 squares with color A and 2 squares with color B.

2. Finish.

Sew the squares together with mattress stitch, turning 1 pair of colors 90° so that their garter ridges run vertically.

Lisa Shobhana Mason is the author of *YarnPlay*. She loves all things handmade — from vintage to modern, kitsch to ultrachic.

Iced Coffee Toddies

Perk up your summer coffee the cold-brewed way.

BY CARLA SINCLAIR

U ntil last year, I avoided iced coffee. It's usually too acidic, and the ice melts immediately in the hot brew, making it weak and watery. I like my coffee strong and smooth, and have always resorted to espresso drinks. Until, that is, the day I stumbled into a café in Maui that proudly served cold-brewed iced "Toddies."

A Toddy (named after Todd Simpson, who invented his cold-brew coffee machine in 1964) is coffee that's been brewed without heat for at least 12 hours. The result is an amazingly smooth, strong, and naturally sweet cup of java without any acidic harshness or bitterness. Although it would be easy to buy the Toddy machine (around $35), here's a low-tech way to cold-brew coffee that's every bit as good as the black gold I discovered in Hawaii.

Photography by Sam Murphy

If you're using a French press, swish your grounds immediately before straining. This will make it easier to press down.

The following method makes a very concentrated coffee. I happen to like it straight, but drinking more than half a glass sends me flying through the roof (unless, of course, it's decaf). It's all a matter of taste, however, and most people seem to prefer diluting this concentrated brew to 1 part coffee, 1 part water, and then pouring it over ice. For an iced latte, keep it concentrated, pour approximately ¼c into a tall glass over ice, then fill the rest up with cold milk.

1. Grind your coffee.

Other recipes claim that inexpensive, medium-coarse ground canned coffee can make a perfect cold-brew coffee. I suggest trying that if you don't mind prepackaged coffee.

Personally, I find that grinding my own beans to a medium-fine ground makes the richest, most flavorful brew. So if you're using your own grinder, grind almost ½c of beans to make ⅓c of medium-fine ground coffee.

2. Soak your grounds.

Pour your grounds and 1½c of water into a glass bowl or French press, gently stir it, cover, and then let the mixture soak for at least 12 hours. I like to do this in the evening so that my coffee is ready in the morning.

3. Filter your coffee.

If you soaked your grounds in a bowl, strain the liquid through a sieve lined with cheesecloth, then strain once more. If using a French press, simply press your coffee. If you find that a bit of coffee sediment remains in your pressed batch of coffee, you can strain it again using a sieve and cheesecloth. (I once used a T-shirt draped across a Mason jar and secured with a rubber band. Paper coffee filters also work.)

4. Pour over ice and serve.

Once your coffee is completely strained, serve up some iced Toddies (remember to dilute with water or milk to taste). Refrigerate leftover coffee in a jar until ready to serve. It stays fresh for at least a week.

❄ **TIP: During those super-hot summer weeks where quick-melting ice can't be avoided, stock your freezer with ice trays filled with coffee rather than water.**

Carla Sinclair is projects editor of CRAFT.

☕ COLD BREW, COAST TO COAST (TO COAST)

Cold-brewed coffee is catching on in cafés from New York to Hawaii. If you need a quick Toddy fix and can't wait for the 12-hour brew, ask your local café for a hit. And then share the news with our readers by posting your own review on forums.craftzine.com. In the meantime, here are a few gems we found.

Blue Bottle Coffee Kiosk
315 Linden Street, San Francisco (510) 653-3394
Weekdays 7 a.m. to 6 p.m., weekends 8 a.m. to 6 p.m.
bluebottlecoffee.net
Wander down a side street in Hayes Valley, and you'll spot true coffee fanatics lined up in front of what looks like a garage. The New Orleans-style cold brew adds a hint of chicory for a velvety chocolate finish. You can also catch Blue Bottle at the Ferry Plaza Farmers Market or at their new café on Mint Street in SOMA.
—Arwen O'Reilly Griffith

Hawaiian Village Coffee
4405 Honoapiilani Highway, Lahaina, Hawaii
(808) 665-1114, 6 a.m. to 9 p.m. daily
hawaiianvillagecoffee.com
Not only is the rich, homemade iced Toddy a must-taste, but this Maui café — jam-packed with Hawaiiana memorabilia — is also a must-see. *—Carla Sinclair*

Intelligentsia Coffee and Tea
Chicago and Los Angeles
Weekdays 6 a.m. to 10 p.m., weekends 7 a.m. to 10 p.m.
intelligentsiacoffee.com
Intelligentsia's coffee is roasted in antique German machines with cast iron drums because contemporary steel roasters don't heat the batch evenly, says Kyle Glanville, Intelligentsia's manager of espresso research and development, and winner of the 2008 U.S. Barista Championship. *—Mark Frauenfelder*

Think Coffee
248 Mercer Street, New York City (212) 228-6226
Weekdays 7:30 a.m. to midnight,
weekends 8 a.m. to midnight
thinkcoffeenyc.com
This airy Washington Square haunt (and haunt it you can, thanks to late hours and free wireless) thinks so highly of its iced coffee that the cup they serve it in proclaims "Think Cold Brewed." They know whereof they speak. *—AG*

➕ You can read (or post your own) reader reviews of cold-brew cafés at forums.craftzine.com.

Intelligentsia

Think Coffee

Photography by Mark Frauenfelder (top) and Arwen O'Reilly Griffith

NO POSTAGE
NECESSARY
IF MAILED
IN THE
UNITED STATES

BUSINESS REPLY MAIL
FIRST-CLASS MAIL PERMIT NO 865 NORTH HOLLYWOOD CA

POSTAGE WILL BE PAID BY ADDRESSEE

Craft:
PO BOX 17046
NORTH HOLLYWOOD CA 91615-9588

NO POSTAGE
NECESSARY
IF MAILED
IN THE
UNITED STATES

BUSINESS REPLY MAIL
FIRST-CLASS MAIL PERMIT NO 865 NORTH HOLLYWOOD CA

POSTAGE WILL BE PAID BY ADDRESSEE

Craft:
PO BOX 17046
NORTH HOLLYWOOD CA 91615-9588

DIY Stilts

Rise above with your own custom pair of stilts.

BY MOLLY GRABER AND CHRIS MERRICK

Photography by Freda Rowley/burningman.com

Have you ever dreamed of being really tall? Walking on stilts is a fun and adventurous sport. But where are you going to get a decent-priced pair of stilts to try for your first time? With these instructions, you can add as much height as you want and not hurt your wallet in the meantime. All you need is the know-how to use some simple tools — or a friend who can help!

Building your own pair of stilts ensures that they're made just for your body, and when you're done you've learned another crafty skill. Then all you'll need is someone to help you learn to walk tall — and also how to fall. It's a blast and we highly recommend it. Stilt walking can be as easy as it looks.

Materials

» **Pair of shoes**
» **Lumber 1½"×1½"** See Step 1 for lengths. Find a straight piece of Douglas fir, ash, or poplar, without bows or knots.
» **½" plywood** cabinet grade, enough for both footplates and C pieces
» **¼" carriage screws: 2½" (4), 4" (2), and 5½" (2)**
» **Flat washers (8)** for carriage screws
» **¼" nylon insert nuts (8)**
» **Wood screws: 1½" (18), ½" (4)**
» **Wood glue**
» **Recycled mountain bike tire**
» **12" zip ties (4)**
» **Foam padding**
» **Strapping material 1"–2" wide** Seatbelt strapping and nylon webbing work well. Get enough to go around your calf, shin guard, foam, and piece B (see Step 1), 1½ times per strap.
» **Velcro** as wide as your strapping. Each strap requires 10" of velcro.
» **D-rings (4)** as wide as your strapping
» **Thread**
» **4" ABS pipe, 14" long**

TOOLS
» **Cordless screwdriver**
» **Drill bits, ¼" and ⅛"**
» **7⁄16" socket wrench**
» **Channel-lock pliers or Vise-Grips**
» **Reciprocating saw or handsaw**
» **Sandpaper**
» **Measuring square** (T square)
» **Jigsaw**
» **Safety glasses**
» **Propane torch**
» **Vise**
» **Heat glove**
» **Sewing machine**
» **Dowel** such as 1" PVC pipe or a broomstick
» **Table saw (optional)**
» **Router, sandpaper (optional)**

DIAGRAM 1

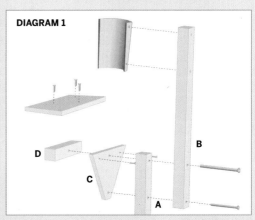

D
C
A
B

■ Animated version at craftzine.com/08/diy_stilts

⚠ **WARNING: When working with power tools, always take safety precautions. Safety glasses are recommended.**

1. Measure and cut wood pieces.
1a. Determine how tall the stilts will be. This will be the length measurement for the pegs (piece A).
1b. Measure from the bottom of your shoe to just below your knee and add 6". This is the length measurement for the shin supports (piece B).
1c. Using a measuring square, cut 2 pieces of 1½"×1½" wood to the length of A and 2 pieces to the length of B. Each stilt needs an extra 7" piece of the 1½"×1½" wood for the foot platform (piece D).
1d. Cut the 2 support trapezoids (piece C) to size and shape from the ½" plywood. Sand all the edges.
1e. Trace the outline of your shoes on ½" plywood and leave at least ½"–¾" extra space outside of the shoe on all sides. The width should be at least 5" across at the middle of the footplate. Cut out both footplates and sand all the edges. Don't trim down the footplate where it will eventually rest against your shin support; this section (the outer edge of each foot) needs to follow a flat, straight line (Figure A).

2. Determine footplate position.
Find your balance by balancing on a dowel. Stand up straight with your feet shoulder-width apart, line up your toes, and find your most comfortable balancing point by rolling the dowel back and forth underneath your feet while looking ahead. When you find the balancing point, have someone mark the outside of your shoes where the shoes intersect the dowel (Figure B). Set the shoes on the footplates and mark each plate to match each shoe (Figure A).

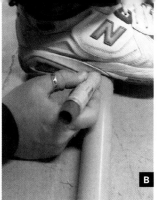
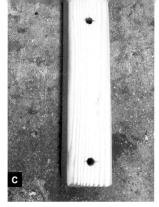

A

B

C

D

E

F

G

H

Fig. A: The footplate follows a straight line against your shin support. Fig. B: Find your balancing point, then mark where the shoes intersect the dowel. Fig. C: Drill holes in piece B with a ¼" bit. Fig. D: Line up A to overlap B by 6". Fig. E: Drill through A using the holes in B as a guide. Fig. F: Using a T square, line up A with C. Fig. G: Use C to guide you as you drill the hole in D. Fig. H: Practice with the carriage bolts on the outside.

3. Drill the wood pieces.

3a. For each stilt, you need pieces A, B, C, and D. Piece A will overlap piece B by 6". Piece C is the next layer, followed by piece D (Diagram 1, previous page). Two bolts go through each of these sets, as shown in Diagram 1. Use caution when drilling the holes: all pieces should be square on top where the footplate will attach.

NOTE: Always label your pieces so that you line them up exactly as you drilled them.

3b. Drill holes in B, as shown in Diagram 1, with a ¼" bit (Figure C).
3c. Line up A to overlap B by 6", including the drilled holes (Figure D). On a flat surface, clamp the 2 pieces together. Drill through A using the holes already drilled in B as a guide (Figure E).
3d. Using a T square, line up A with C (Figure F). Clamp together and use the holes already drilled in A to guide you as you drill the holes in C.
3e. Line up D with C and use a T square for the top edge. Clamp and use C to guide you as you drill the hole in D (Figure G).

4. Assemble the wood pieces.

4a. Practice assembling (Diagram 1), with the heads of the 5½" and 4" carriage bolts on the outside of the assembly (Figure H). If the pieces fit and form a flat rest for your footplate, take them apart and reassemble them, gluing each joint as you go. Holding the head of the bolt with pliers, tighten the nuts with a ⁷⁄₁₆" wrench so the bolts sink into the wood. Pre-drill and screw 2 wood screws through C, attaching it to D.
4b. Pay attention to how the footplate will attach for each stilt (Figure I). Arrange the pieces for each stilt so that B is on the outside of the shin. Pre-drill and attach the footplate to D and A with wood screws (Figure J).

5. Prepare and attach shin guards.

5a. Cut 2 pieces of your ABS pipe to 6" lengths with a reciprocating saw or handsaw. Cut out a 3"-wide vertical section of each with a jigsaw (Figure K).
5b. Clamp the ABS pipe in a vise, heat the middle section with a propane torch, and using a glove, gently bend the ABS to flare out to the shape of your shin. Once you think the ABS is bent out enough to fit around your shin with foam padding set inside, let

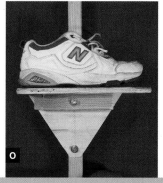
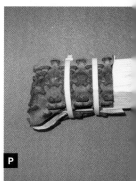

Fig. I: Each footplate sits on the peg so that the shin support is on the outside the shin. Fig. J: Pre-drill and attach the footplate with wood screws. Fig. K: Cut out a 3"-wide vertical section of each ABS piece. Fig. L: Fit the ABS and the foam to your shin. Fig. M: Swing the front of the shin plate toward piece A so that it shows 1¼" past piece B. Fig. N: Attach straps. Fig. O: Test the balance before attaching the shoes. Fig. P: Peg footing from a bike tire.

it cool, then hold the ABS and the foam to your shin to make sure they fit (Figure L). You may have to heat and bend it again so that it fits well.

5c. Drill a hole with the ¼" bit 1" from the top of B. Use that hole to guide you in drilling your first hole in the ABS shin plate. Then thread the top hole of B and the ABS with a 2½" carriage bolt (this time with the head facing inward toward your shin), but don't tighten it. Swing the front of the shin plate toward A so that it shows 1¼" past B (Figure M). Drill the bottom hole through A and the shin plate. Thread holes with a 2½" carriage bolt. Tighten both bolts. Trim excess ABS and bolt material with a reciprocating saw.

⚠ **WARNING: If you don't have much experience using a reciprocating saw, ask someone for help on this step.**

6. Sew straps and attach the foam.

6a. The strap wraps around the back of your calf to the front, through the D-ring, and attaches back to itself with velcro (Figure N). Sew the strap to the D-ring and the velcro to the strap.

6b. Pre-drill the holes. Use ½" wood screws to attach the straps to A on the upper end adjacent to the shin plate with the D-ring facing forward.

6c. Cut a 7"×15" piece of foam padding. Glue the foam onto your shin plates so that it wraps around the outside and back of your calf. Sew fabric around the foam for comfort, if you like.

7. Attach shoes and footings.

7a. Arrange each shoe on each footplate so the mark on the outside of the shoe lines up with the line on your footplate and with the middle of A. Stand on your stilts with your shoes on to find the right shoe placement before attaching them (Figure O).

7b. Loosen laces and remove shoe liners. Pre-drill and screw each shoe onto a footplate with at least 2 wood screws per shoe.

7c. Use zip ties to attach the bike tire footings to the bottom of the stilts (Figure P).

➕ For more information, check out vigilantiup.org.

Molly Graber is an environmental biologist who enjoys gardening, hiking, and stilt walking with friends at festivals. Chris Merrick, an electrical engineer by day, inventor at night, and tinkerer for life, can do almost anything with his hands.

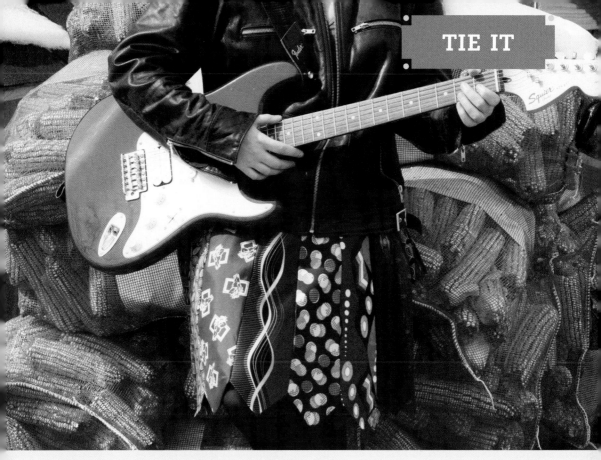

Tie One On

Fashion a playful skirt from new and used neckties. BY SALLY L. CONVERSE-DOUCETTE

S o many cool ties, but who wants to wear them around their neck? Why not sew them together to make a funky skirt?

A couple months ago a friend gave me a fabulous collection of vintage and not-so-vintage neckties. Thrilled, I sorted out the ties that were too fragile and those with spots or stains, and organized the remainders to make 3 skirts. My tie skirts are fun to wear and have started some great conversations. Gather a handful of neckties and some simple supplies, and you too can tie on a unique and eye-catching skirt.

+ TIE IT: NECKTIE SKIRT

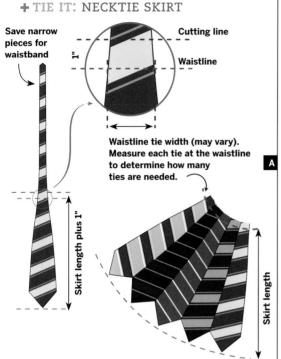

Save narrow pieces for waistband

Cutting line

Waistline

1"

Waistline tie width (may vary). Measure each tie at the waistline to determine how many ties are needed.

Skirt length plus 1"

Skirt length

A **B**

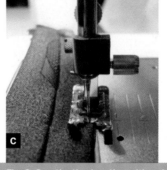

C **D**

Fig. A: Measure the desired length of your skirt. Then determine how many ties you need based on your waistline measurement. Fig. B: Arrange your ties so that you're satisfied with the overall look of the assembly.

Fig. C: Sew the ties together with a zigzag stitch, making sure to catch the edges of both ties. Fig. D: Press the seam open.

Materials

- » **Neckties** See Step 2 to figure out how many you'll need.
- » **Black sewing thread**
- » **Sewing scissors**
- » **Sewing machine** with the ability to zigzag
- » **Measuring tape**
- » **Pins**
- » **Hand-sewing needle**
- » **¼" twill tape** enough to go around your waist plus 8"–10"
- » **Iron**

1. Find your ties.

Of course, retail stores sell ties, but it's more fun and less expensive to shop at used clothing stores, the Salvation Army, and other charity shops. Don't overlook ties you may already have around the house. It's important to check for stains, holes, and durability. Choose clean and sturdy ties.

2. Measure.

The number of ties needed for your skirt depends on your waist size and the width of your ties. Measure down from your waist to get the desired length of your skirt. Use this number to measure up from the bottom front tip of your tie. The width of this upper part of the tie, minus ⅛" for seam allowance, is how much fabric the tie adds to the waist measurement of your skirt. The total measured width of your ties needs to add up to your waist measurement plus 8"–10" for an overlap (Figure A).

3. Plan your skirt.

After you've selected your ties, find a large, flat area to lay them out. Arrange and rearrange them until you're satisfied with the overall look and effect of the tie assembly (Figure B).

4. Sew your ties together.

4a. Cut the ties to your desired length (as discussed in Step 2) plus 1".

4b. Arrange the ties to your liking, keeping in mind that the skirt will overlap 8"–10" at the front, right side over left.

Illustration by Sally Converse-Doucette

Fig. E: Sew several leftover narrow tie pieces together to form 1 long piece for the waistband. Fig. F: Start pinning the waistband to the waistline.

Fig. G: Sew along the edge of the waistband that touches the twill tape. Fig. H: Press the waistband up over the seam allowance.

4c. Starting with either end of the skirt, place the first and second ties face to face and pin along the sewing edge. Set the sewing machine to a very narrow zigzag and stitch down the edge of the ties, making sure to catch the edges of both ties (Figure C). Press open (Figure D). Repeat this process, adding ties in the proper order until they are all sewn together.

4d. At the waist, stitch 1" in from the edge. Pin ¼" twill tape over this stitching to reinforce the waist, and stitch in place using a narrow zigzag. Trim the waist edge, leaving a ⅝" seam allowance. Finish the edge using a wide zigzag or other finishing stitch.

5. Assemble the waistband.
Sew several leftover narrow tie pieces together to form 1 long piece that measures 2 times the waist measurement plus 1yd (Figure E). Use uncut, pointed edges for both ends of the waistband. These ends will form sashes at either side of the waistband.

6. Attach the waistband.
Place the waistband facedown on the front of skirt. Start pinning the waistband to the waistline, just touching the lower side of the twill tape on the skirt's right front side (Figure F). Leave an 18" piece of waistband hanging free to serve as the right front skirt sash, and pin around the waistline of the skirt. There will be some extra waistband that extends beyond the left side of the skirt; this will partially wrap around the waist and serve as the left end of the sash.

Using a narrow zigzag stitch, sew along the edge of the waistband that touches the twill tape (Figure G). Press the waistband up over the seam allowance (Figure H). Hand-stitch the back of the waistband to the seam allowance.

7. Finish.
Wrap the skirt around your waist so that the right front overlaps the left. Mark the waistband at the left side with a pin. Sew a 1¼" buttonhole centered over the pin. Cut the buttonhole open and pass the waistband sash through the buttonhole from under the waistband to the top of the skirt. Tie and enjoy!

Sally Converse-Doucette is an artist with a B.F.A. in fine arts and theatre design. She owns her own graphic design company, slixgrfx, specializing in web design.

Necktie Glasses Case

Fashion a stylish carrying case from a great old tie.

BY DIANE GILLELAND

A thrift store necktie is the perfect raw material for a carrying case: it's elegant and comes with its own padding to protect your valuables. Plus, you need only a few minutes and a little hand-sewing to whip one up. Although this project shows you how to make a case for eyeglasses, they're also great for crochet hooks, scissors, business cards, and pens.

Photography by Diane Gilleland

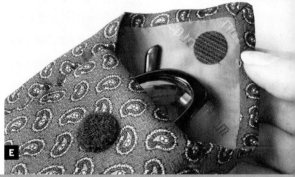

Fig. A: Fold the necktie over your glasses and cut the tie about 1" past the top of the glasses. Fig. B: Fold the cut edge to the inside twice, and hem with a tiny whipstitch. Fig. C: Starting at the pointed end, carefully remove enough of the center back seam to accommodate your glasses. Remove any labels as well. Fig. D: Fold the tie, matching the hemmed edge with the base of the pointed tip. Pin in place. Fig. E: Glue on a velcro dot closure.

Materials

» **Necktie** preferably not too skinny
» **Sewing needle**
» **Coordinating thread**
» **Scissors**
» **Seam ripper**
» **Button** 1" or larger
» **Set of ½" velcro dots**
» **Fabric glue**

1. Measure your case.

Lay the necktie flat, backside facing up. Place your folded glasses on top. The top of the glasses should line up with the inside of the tie as shown in Figure A. Fold the rest of the tie over the glasses, and cut it so it extends 1" beyond the top of the glasses.

2. Finish the cut edge.

Fold 1" of the cut edge toward the back of the tie and whipstitch it in place (Figure B). If the tie's internal padding sticks out, turn that under as you stitch.

3. Open up the inside.

Most ties are made with a hand-sewn center seam — you'll need to remove some of this seam in order to fit things inside your case. Use a seam ripper to remove the stitching (Figure C). You only need to remove enough stitching to accommodate your glasses. If your tie has a label, remove this too.

4. Sew the side seams.

Set your glasses aside and fold the tie as shown in Figure D. Pin the 2 layers together and hand-sew them along both sides with a hemstitch or a tiny whipstitch. Stitch only through the topmost layers of fabric — you don't want to sew the front and back of your case together!

5. Add a closure.

Fold the tip of the tie over to make a flap. Sew a button on the outside of this flap. Glue velcro dots under the button to hold your case closed. Once the glue is dry, your glasses are good to go (Figure E).

Diane Gilleland produces CraftyPod, a blog and podcast about making stuff. craftypod.com

Polaroid Transfer-mations

Create the appearance of an antique image with this simple process. BY ABI COTLER O'ROARTY

For those who still long for a tangible connection with film photographs, Polaroid transfers can transform ordinary photos into Impressionist masterpieces. With a Daylab slide printer or old Polaroid Land camera, you can easily turn your favorite old slide images into framable pieces of art.

The process is fairly simple: Polaroid negatives are rubbed (transferred) onto textured watercolor paper (or other materials, if you're so inspired). The resulting ethereal images appear to be antiques from their weathered appearance. And because the look is almost ghostly, even unintentional "mistakes" may become your favorites.

NOTE: Polaroid announced it would stop manufacturing film in April 2008, but Fuji makes a comparable film called Fuji FP-100C.

Atomic Robot 2 Polaroid transfer by Jennifer Kennard / Corbis

Fig. A: Insert your slide into the Daylab to convert it to a Polaroid print (with negative). Fig. B: Prep the paper by soaking it in warm water. Fig. C: Remove the paper after at least 1 minute. Fig. D: Pull the Polaroid apart to reveal its print side and its negative side (the black one). Fig. E: Roll the negative onto the paper to transfer the image; wait 2 minutes before lifting off the negative. Fig. F: The proud finished product.

Photography by Abi Cotler O'Roarty

Materials

» **An old slide** or a newly taken one!
» **Daylab CopySystem Pro slide printer or Polaroid Land camera** The Land camera is no longer made but can be found on eBay for as little as $5.
» **Instant photo film** Polaroid 669 or 559 or Fuji FP-100C
» **Hot-press watercolor paper**
» **Brayer or roller**
» **Photo tray** for paper
» **Optional: Hair dryer, white vinegar**

1. For the Daylab, find a slide.

If using a slide, insert it into the Daylab to create a print (Figure A). If using a Polaroid, skip this step.

2. Prep the paper.

Soak watercolor paper in warm water until it's soft, around 1 minute (Figure B). Remove it from the water (Figure C) and pat it dry.

3. Make your Polaroid.

If using a Daylab, expose the Polaroid film; if using a Polaroid camera, take your shot. The image stays latent until it's pulled. Pull the processing tab on the film, pulling the film through the rollers with one smooth motion. After 15 seconds of developing, pull apart the 2 sides of the Polaroid film (Figure D).

4. Reveal your image.

Pull away the negative and set it facedown on your wet paper. Careful not to let it slide, firmly roll the brayer on the back (Figure E). Wait about 2 minutes. You need heat from the developing negative to warm the paper, so a hair dryer may help. Slowly lift the negative off the paper by a corner (Figure F).

5. Optional wash.

Polaroid chemistry is basic (alkaline), so it helps to stabilize the image if you soak the transfer in a weak acid. Try 1 part white vinegar to 4 parts water, for no more than 1 minute, with some agitation. Then rinse in running water for 4 minutes and allow to air-dry.

Abi O'Roarty teaches at the Art Institute of California, San Diego, and freelances from her home in Cardiff-by-the-Sea.

1

Shoot for the Stars

With a few helpful hints, you can shoot like the pros. BY ABI COTLER O'ROARTY

Most new digital cameras are able to compensate for human error in different ways. But the art of composing a good shot requires a bit of firsthand knowledge. Here we offer you 10 tips used by professional photographers (and corresponding sample photos) that will help you achieve not just a good photograph, but a great one. Don't worry if you don't remember them all every time you take a photo. Your growing knowledge of photography will build on itself as you continue to delve in further. Most importantly, have fun! There's a wealth of award-winning images out there still waiting to be shot.

Photography by Natalia Chocron

Fig. 2: Always check the background of your subject to make sure there are no distractions. Here, where the child is the focus, the blurred shrubs makes a nice backdrop. Fig. 3: Using your Macro or Flower mode can give a big impact to small subects. Fig. 4: A subject that is off-center usually makes a more interesting composition. Fig. 5: Ensure that your subject is the sharpest image in the photo by locking the focus with your shutter button.

1. Make wise digital decisions.

If you're shooting digital (and we're assuming you are), don't compromise quality — capture all the pixels you can. It's the amount of pixels per square inch that gives quality to your images, and you wouldn't want to take an award-winning shot that can only be enlarged to the size of a credit card. So always shoot at your camera's highest possible resolution.

2. Showcase your subject.

Decide what you're really taking a picture of, and center your efforts on taking the best possible photo of this subject, be it a person, place, thing, or even mood. Be sure to keep anything that would distract out of the picture. Also check the area behind the subject, looking for trees or phone poles sprouting from a person's head. Remember, a clean background will emphasize your subject and have a stronger visual impact.

3. Get close, then get closer.

Try to zoom or move in to fill the frame with your subject, and don't be afraid to get close — really close. That way you can truly make an impact. Even cutting into the subject a bit can be dynamic

and lend the image an intimate mood. Use the Macro or Flower mode for small subjects. Even the simplest object takes on new fascination in Macro mode.

4. Strive for dynamic compositions.

One of the most important aspects of composition is the Rule of Thirds. The concept, discovered by the Greeks, is simple. Imagine a tic-tac-toe grid across your frame, and place the subject at 1 of the 4 line intersections. This doesn't mean that there isn't a time and place when you want to center your subject (an image highlighting perfect symmetry comes to mind). But usually, the strongest and most visually interesting place for your subject is at 1 of these 4 points.

5. Lock that focus.

Most cameras focus on whatever is in the middle of the frame. As we just learned, that's rarely the best place for your subject, so it may be out of focus. To combat this, center the subject and press the shutter button down halfway to lock in the focus. Then reframe the picture and press the shutter button all the way to take the shot with perfect sharpness.

Fig. 6: The photo on the right was taken with a polarizer, a camera filter used in outdoor photography that reduces glare and gives you more saturated colors. Polarizers work with all types of cameras.

Fig. 7: In-camera meters automatically try to make your subject 18% gray, but sometimes the subject is too light or dark for this to work well (photos on the left). We used a "gray-balancing" card to get the image on the right.

6. Try a polarizer.

A polarizer is one filter every photographer should have for general outdoor shooting. It works with both single-lens reflex cameras and point-and-shoots (just by holding the polarizer in front of the lens). By reducing glare, the polarizer gives your shots richer, more saturated colors, especially with skies (see the before and after shots above). Just one caveat: polarizers give such nice saturation by eliminating reflections, so be sure not to use one if you're actually trying to capture a reflection image.

7. Trick your auto-exposure.

In-camera meters try to make your subject 18% gray. But some subjects are vastly darker or lighter than that, so it's easy for your meter to get tricked and turn a snowy hillside into a dark, muddy mess. What you need to do is trick your meter back.

The most reliable way to do this is to use an 18% gray card like the one made by Kodak. To use it, place the card in the same light as your subject. Then point your camera at it, filling the frame. Lock in this exposure by pressing the shutter button halfway, then recompose and shoot with perfect exposure still set.

If you don't have a gray card, do the same thing

with something in the scene that seems 18% gray. This may be your own hand, a rock, or the grass in the same light as your subject.

8. Master outdoor lighting.

For stellar outdoor shooting, use these tips for the 3 main times of day:

» **Middle of the day** Harsh midday sunlight is especially problematic, because of dark shadows in the eye sockets, under the nose, and in other unflattering crags. A terrific solution is your camera's Fill Flash mode, where the camera exposes for the background first, then adds just enough flash to illuminate your subject. Use Fill Flash midday to lighten dark shadows and even on cloudy days to brighten faces and separate them from the background.

» **Early/late day** For scenic shots, the light is usually best very early or very late in the day. That's when you get the warm tones and long shadows of professional nature work. Of course, people and animals also look great in this light. You can even experiment with Fill Flash to balance a glowing sidelight from the sun where the face is mostly in shadow.

» **End of day/Magic Hour** The part of the day

Fig 8: For supreme lighting, outdoor shots are best taken in the morning or very late in the day. If shooting in midday, you should probably set your camera to Fill Flash to reduce harshness. This photo was taken at 12 noon.

Fig. 9: Indoor shooting can be tricky with lighting, but a north-facing window gives flattering light. Fig. 10: Playing with your AV (left image) and TV (right image) modes will change the focus of a moving subject.

when the sun has just set or is just about to rise is known as Magic Hour. Its brightly diffused light is the darling of photographers of car ads and other hard-to-light surfaces. This even, pinkish light is also terrific for shooting people. (A similarly flattering light is that of cloudy days. A bride may be unhappy about an overcast nuptial day, but the wedding photographer never is.)

9. Master indoor lighting.

Indoor photography can be especially tricky, so remember these tips:

» Without a flash, indoor lighting lends a funny color cast to your images. To correct this, set your white balance if shooting digital. If using film, buy the type that's balanced for your type of room lighting.

» To combat harsh shadows from an indoor flash, try covering it with diffusion material. Even bathroom tissue or a white T-shirt works.

» Light from a north-facing window can be exceptionally flattering. Try a "window-light" portrait, in which a person (or object) is placed next to a window without direct sunlight coming through and then, often, turned to the side so that only part of the face is illuminated by the window's even light.

10. Understand program modes.

To control certain aspects of your exposure in order to produce desired effects, take the camera out of automatic or P mode, and try the other exposure modes:

» **A or AV (aperture value) mode** This allows you to set the aperture while the camera sets the appropriate shutter speed. You might use AV mode to lower the shutter speed to create a shallow depth of field (like f/4.0), which will blur the background and result in clean, snappy portraits.

» **TV (time value) mode** Here, you control the shutter speed and the camera sets the aperture. You might use TV mode when you know you need at least 1/1000 to capture a flock of bicyclists as they fly by your lens, but you want the camera to decide the appropriate aperture for that speed.

In both these cases, if there isn't enough light to compensate, your image may still be underexposed. This will usually be signified by a flashing number in your camera's LCD screen where exposure is read.

Dear Susan,

Thank you so much for the wonderful ha
bag everyday for my errands and think

xoxo,
Natalie

Computer Cursive
Create your own digital handwriting font.

BY NATALIE ZEE DRIEU

In my youth, I loved everything about the art of writing, spending hours improving my handwriting and even learning the art of calligraphy. Even today, I have nice penmanship, but oftentimes jotting down a quick note ends up as an illegible nightmare. I'm out of practice! Like most people these days, I spend way too much time typing on a keyboard rather than writing with a pen. But we are living in the digital world, right?

Enter the Fontifier (fontifier.com), where you can create a digital typeface from your own handwriting. For $9, you'll be able to add a personal touch to your digital photos and craft projects without lifting a pen. I'll be the first to admit my handwriting is no art form, like others I know, but it's mine with its own special curves and curls.

Photograph by Sam Murphy

Fontifier // Your own handwriting on your computer!

www.fontifier.com

A	B	C	D	E	F	G	H	I	J	K
A	B	C	D	E	F	G	H	I	J	K
L	M	N	O	P	Q	R	S	T	U	V
L	M	N	O	P	Q	R	S	T	U	V
W	X	Y	Z	&	!	?	$	¢	£	€
W	X	Y	Z	&	!	?	$	¢	£	€
a	b	c	d	e	f	g	h	i	j	k
a	b	c	d	e	f	g	h	i	j	k
l	m	n	o	p	q	r	s	t	u	v
l	m	n	o	p	q	r	s	t	u	v
w	x	y	z	.	,	:	;	-	'	"
w	x	y	z	.	,	:	;	-	'	"
0	1	2	3	4	5	6	7	8	9	@
0	1	2	3	4	5	6	7	8	9	@
(	)	[	]	<	>	{	}	/	\	|
(	)	[	]	<	>	{	}	/	\	|
+	±	*	=	¬	~	^	#	%	`	–
+	±	*	=	¬	~	^	#	%	`	–

Fig. A: Write each letter in the appropriate box with a black felt pen. The tick marks on the sides of each box represent the baseline.

Fig. B: Scan your template in, and then make adjustments as necessary using an image editing tool such as Photoshop.

Materials

» Computer
» Printer
» Scanner
» Printer paper
» Adobe Photoshop or other image editing tool (optional)
» Black felt-tip pen

1. Print the template.

Go to fontifier.com and print out the template.

2. Start writing.

Using a black felt-tip pen, fill in the letters or symbols in each box, making sure to give each letter breathing room on the sides (Figure A). The little tick marks on the sides of each box should be considered the baseline for each letter. Just remember, the thicker your pen is, the thicker your font weight will be. Using a pen that's too thin will result in a very lightweight font that could be hard to read.

3. Scan in the template.

On the scanner, scan in the entire template, making sure to include the outer border. Save the graphic as a .gif, .jpeg, .png, or .tiff file at 72, 75, or 100dpi.

4. Make little fixes in Photoshop (optional).

I spend most of my time typing rather than writing, and if your handwriting is like mine — characters aren't even or well aligned — you can do some modifying in Photoshop or use your preferred image editing tool.

To do this, bring the scanned template into Photoshop and use the line rulers to match the baseline marks of each letter. Once you have those set, you can align each letter to the bottom of your line ruler, or scale a letter so that it looks even with the others (Figure B).

5. Upload your template.

Once you've got all the letters and symbols to your liking, upload your template to Fontifier. You'll be able to preview the font and a sample sentence to see if you like it before you purchase.

Preview font

Preview of **Natalie's-Handwriting.ttf**:

The quick brown fox

jumps over a lazy dog.
ABCDEFGHIJKLMNOPQRSTUVWXYZ&!?$¢£€

abcdefghi jklmnopqrstuvwxyz.,:;-'"

0123456789@()[]<>{}/\|+±#=¬~^#%`_

When you are happy with your preview, buy your font and download it for $9 US.

Please select your preferred secure payment method:

(Pay by Credit Card)   (Pay by PayPal)

C

6. Name your font.

My font is named "Natalie's Handwriting." You'll also need to enter your full name in the box below it for copyright information for your font.

7. Preview your font.

Check to see if your characters are legible and well aligned (Figure C). If you don't like this preview, tweak them some more and upload a new template.

8. Purchase and download.

If the preview is to your liking, click the purchase button to pay by either credit card or PayPal.

Immediately after purchasing, you can download your finished font! Install it in your computer's font folder and use it in your word and graphics programs, such as Word or Photoshop.

If you're looking to create a whole font family with boldface and italic versions, it's an extra $9 for each of these. You may find it's more fun to make a variety of writing styles for your craft projects.

One thing to keep in mind is that your font is a bitmap (not vector) version of your handwriting, so the edges may look jagged at larger font sizes. Use it for your digital photos, cards, or little notes.

Play around and have fun with it!

ABCDEFGHIJKLM
NOPQRSTUVWXYZ

abcdefghi jklm
nopqrstuvwxyz

0123456789

!@#$%^&*()_+:{}\?

The quick brown fox
jumps over a lazy dog.

Natalie Zee Drieu is senior editor of CRAFT and writes for the CRAFT blog at craftzine.com.

Shoot the Rainbow BY MAGGIE STEWART

❖❖ My housemates and I were planning a party, and we decided that an excellent drinking game would involve shooting all the colors of the rainbow. And thus, Skittles Vodka was born.

YOU WILL NEED:

» **Five 750ml bottles of good-quality vodka**
  or 1 large bottle and 5 empty jars
» **2lbs (900g) of Skittles candy**
» **Cheesecloth or paper towels**
» **Strainer**
» **Mixers (optional)**

1. Sort and count the Skittles.

Sort the Skittles into bowls by color. You need 180g of each color, and since Skittles are about 1.125g each, that's 160 Skittles. You can add more Skittles for more flavor.

We found that medium-quality vodka ended up tasting like medicine (particularly the cherry flavor), so use a better- or high-quality vodka. We used one 750ml bottle for each flavor.

2. Create the potion.

Pour out and reserve ⅛ of the vodka from each bottle. Drop the Skittles by color into each bottle, then top off with the reserved vodka. (Enjoy the leftovers at your leisure.)

Alternatively, put the Skittles into 5 separate jars and pour equal amounts of vodka into them. Give each bottle a good shake and set them aside overnight to dissolve the candy.

3. Filter out the candy residue.

Besides sugar and flavoring, Skittles contain some lovely filler. This is the white stuff that ends up floating on top. It's pretty horrible, so it needs to be filtered out. We filtered the liquid through several layers of paper towels pushed down into a strainer. It takes a while, and the stuff left behind is pretty gross, but it's worth it.

4. Enjoy straight or with mixers.

I liked the green flavor best — it was the closest to the original Skittle flavor. Red tasted like cough syrup. Try mixing orange with club soda over ice for a refreshing, summery drink.

Maggie Stewart lives in the Garden State, yet totally fails to garden. Instead she bakes, makes candy, and fiddles with alcoholic beverages.

Photography by Ed Troxell and Sam Murphy (final shot)

Craft: Collection

» The **CRAFT: Collection** is our new fashion feature, showcasing just a few of our favorite independent and DIY designers.

Dress Up From vintage styles to modern cuts,
here's a fresh take on the dresses of the season.

SEW IT!

MINNA DRESS **BurdaStyle**
» **Free pattern at** burdastyle.com

HALTER BUBBLE DRESS **New York Couture**
» newyorkcouture.net

VINTAGE LACE FELTED WOOL DRESS **Ashley Rose Helvey** » ashleyrosehelvey.blogspot.com

ABSTRACT FLOWER MOTIF DRESS **Dadadress** » dadadress.com

SPRING LEMONSTORY DRESS **Lemonstory by Kianna** » kimenna.etsy.com

MODERN RUFFLE DRESS **Liza Rietz** » lizarietz.com

101:

BONSAI

By Brookelynn Morris

Miniaturize your favorite tree with this ancient art.

Bonsai plants are, in their essence, little trees. Yet the art of bonsai has a much greater scope: it strives to replicate nature. It is an art that emulates the elements and their action on living plants. A tree is just a sapling until the roots grow, the water comes into the soil, and the forces of sun, wind, and gravity sculpt it into shape. The bonsai artist uses a variety of tools to replicate these effects and create a perfect miniature version of life on Earth.

Watching your tiny tree as it cycles through the seasons, going dormant, pushing out leaf buds, blossoming, and then producing fruits or berries is very rewarding, and a wonderful way to connect with the natural world.

»

Photography by Nat Wilson-Heckathorn

BASICS »

The art of growing bonsai is well adapted to the urban gardener. These plantings require less water, less soil, and less square footage. But just because they're diminutive, doesn't mean that they don't need great amounts of care and tending. Regular waterings are the most essential. Tasks such as repotting and restyling are done when needed, as well as pruning, training, and shaping. These chores are not without reward. Because bonsai can recreate complete landscapes, the impression of grand natural space exudes from these small displays.

Aesthetics dominate the art of bonsai. Many stringent rules exist for the purists dedicated to this art. Ancient standards declare that certain trees are to be grown in certain shapes and planted into certain pots. But the modern, creative gardener follows her own path toward beauty. Just be sure to never lose sight of the visual appeal and design of your plantings.

The more you learn about bonsai, the more you realize what you have yet to learn. To properly cultivate a design could take decades. From the beginning, art is made and life is growing, but the passage of time is the core of bonsai. Many experts in the field have been growing bonsai 50 years or more. This is a simple primer to help you establish your roots.

MATERIALS

- » Sapling
- » Soil mix, Small rocks
- » Screen
- » Pottery
- » Small rake, Fine shears
- » Copper wire
- » Hemp twine
- » Water
- » Fertilizer, various types and strengths
- » Moss, pebbles, other plants (optional)

BONSAI STYLES

Bonsai are often classified into five basic styles — *formal upright*, *informal upright*, *slanting*, *cascade*, and *semi-cascade* — based on the overall shape and how much the trunk slants. You'll also find dozens of additional styles such as *literati*, *windswept*, and *weeping branch*, which you can mix and modify as you see fit. A good introduction can be found at craftzine. com/go/bonsai or in *Bonsai for Beginners* by Craig Coussins (Sterling Publishing).

START »

1. CHOOSE YOUR TREE

Choosing the species of tree to grow is the first, and possibly most difficult, task. Pines and maples are perhaps the most recognizable bonsai. These trees are classic beauties and well suited for miniaturization. Flowering and fruiting trees are popular as well, especially the quince and pomegranate.

But bonsai trees are not necessarily always trees. Many shrubs can be grown and manipulated into bonsai forms that belie their natural state. Wisteria vines and azaleas can be shaped into thick tree trunks that they would never produce normally.

The tree can be grown from seed or propagated through a cutting. The easiest way to begin is to select a sapling from your favorite nursery (Figure A).

A

2. SELECT A COMPLEMENTARY CONTAINER

The chosen tree will dictate its container. The two must make a visually pleasing combination. Traditionally, the intended shape of the tree is matched to a specific pot. For instance, a straight-sided pot would be used for a straight-growing formal upright style tree (Figure B), while a round or oval pot would be used for an informal style with a curving trunk or limbs. The same rules state that evergreens should be exclusively set into unglazed containers.

While there is room for variance, in general you'll find that your eye will naturally follow some of these same rules of design out of instinct. When choosing a pot, consider the sides and consider the depth. If you're growing a tree that will cascade out of the pot like it's growing on the edge of a cliff, you'll want to choose a tall pot; a collective planting meant to look like a meadow needs a wide and shallow one.

Finally, select the hue of the pottery. Try to complement the color of the leaves most of all.

B

3. PREPARE THE SOIL

Dirt is a tree's lifeline. The soil clinging to the roots provides the tree with its moisture and nutrients. It is crucial to use a mix that will hold water, but not keep the roots too wet. The grain of the soil is also a consideration. When a tree's root encounters a large, sharp rock, the tip of the root splits in two and grows around it. The result is a finer, thinner root, unable to take up as much water as a large root, therefore contributing to natural miniaturization.

Plant your bonsai tree in soil with a combination of rich dirt and larger bits of rock to replicate this effect (Figure C). You can purchase specialty soil, custom-tailored to suit the unique texture and drainage needs of bonsai, or you can customize your own soil with raw materials such as bark, coconut fiber, perlite, and rock chips.

C

4. PLANT THE BONSAI

4a. If the pot does not have drainage holes, use a drill with a ceramic bit to add a hole. To prevent soil loss, cover it with a piece of screen (Figure D).

4b. Before planting, gently remove the tree from its container and inspect the roots. They will likely have grown around each other. Pull loose these tangled, skinny roots with your hands, and trim away the shaggy ends with hand shears. Also remove any brown or unhealthy roots. *Next, find the taproot (the primary root), and cut it off. This is an important step to dwarf the plant.* Finally, fan out and thin the roots at the base of the trunk using the rake (Figure E). Always use a gentle touch with the roots.

4c. Cover the bottom of the pot with soil. Add the tree with its roots fanned out wide. Cover the roots with soil, filling the pot evenly until the surface of the dirt is level (Figure F). Now give the tree a generous drink, to "water it in" (Figure G). Finally, add any moss, rocks, or companion plants to flesh out your design (Figure H).

5. TEND THE BONSAI

5a. Place the tree in direct sunlight. If the light seems too intense for young or delicate trees, hang a shade cloth to filter the light. Water as needed. Do not put your tree on a strict schedule. Wait for it to become mostly dry before you water.

5b. Maintain the health of the tree, and begin to shape it, with simple pruning and pinching. Prune any branches that are less than healthy, or that stand in the way of the shape you'd like to make (Figure I). Pinching back new growth at the ends of branches will encourage thickening.

5c. Before you start shaping the tree, allow it to grow until it seems well established in its new environment. Depending on your patience, this might be a season, or a whole year, or only a few weeks.

5d. Feed the bonsai throughout the year. During winter dormancy, feed it a fertilizer low in nitrogen. When spring arrives, increase the amount of nitrogen, and through the summer use a balanced food.

6. SHAPE THE BONSAI

When shaping trees, the objective is to manipulate the tree, without scarring the bark, to create the illusion of years of natural stress from the forces of nature. Start slow, with gentle tension. You can gradually increase the tension over time. Here are 3 methods:

» Wire. When wiring, use care not to damage the tree. Don't wrap the wire too tightly around the wood. Check the wiring often, removing and replacing it as the tree grows. Begin by coiling one end of the copper wire around the base of the tree, and wind it along the trunk or branch you wish to bend (Figure J). Be certain to lay the wire evenly so as to properly distribute the pressure. When the tree has been wired, bend the branch or trunk carefully with both hands, gripping evenly to avoid snapping the tree.

» Tie. Tie a piece of thin hemp rope or cotton twine around the pot. Now tie a piece of twine to the branch you wish to bend, and pull it down with the string until it curves as you like. To maintain the tension, tie the loose end to the string that's tied around the pot (Figure K).

» Weight. Choose a small stone, not heavy enough to break the tree, and hang it from the trunk or branch with a small length of wire or string. Don't hang the weight from the very tip, as you could break the tree. Instead, start 1/3 of the way from the tip, wrap the wire or string evenly around until you reach the end, and then let the stone dangle (Figure L).

Depending on the thickness of the trunk, and the shape you intend to create, you might use these techniques over the course of a season, or even for a year or more.

FINISH ⊠

Brookelynn Morris lives in NorCal and loves to grow. Her garden right now includes climbing roses, English roses, four kinds of clematis, red sunflowers, dusty miller, abutilon, raspberries, foxgloves, lots of succulents, and herbs.

DISPLAYING BONSAI

Potting a perfect tree into a perfect pot is not the final step. This art must be displayed, and thus honored. Placing the tree on a small stand gives it a sense of importance, and elevates it above the common. Consider something simple, such as a piece of cork, a modest wooden plant stand with short legs that doesn't throw off the balance, a slab of raw slate, or a lacquered tray.

IT'S A ...

SLED ON A **THREAD**!

GLAD THOSE KIDS TOLD US TO "GO FLY A KITE!"

I NEVER THOUGHT THEY'D TAKE US LITERALLY.

Photograph by Cody Pickens

THE SIMPLEST AND EASIEST MATERIAL FOR KITE MAKING IS TYVEK. IT DOESN'T REQUIRE STITCHING, JUST TYVEK TAPE, WHICH CAN BE PURCHASED IN HARDWARE STORES OR FOUND AT CONSTRUCTION SITES. THE OTHER MATERIALS YOU'LL NEED ARE ...

CRAFT MAGAZINE

YARDSTICK

WASHER

TYVEK TAPE

STRING. THE THINNEST, STRONGEST LINE IS BEST. NYLON OR FISHING LINE WILL WORK IN A PINCH.

SCISSORS

MEASURE AND DRAW OUT THE FOLLOWING PIECES ACCURATELY TO THESE PROPORTIONS.

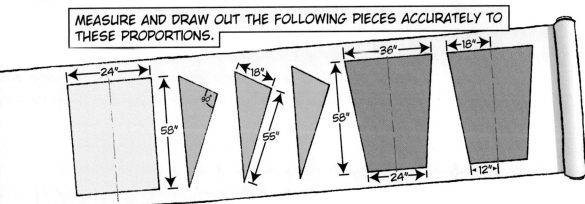

ONCE IT'S LAID OUT, GET TO DECORATING. TYVEK MAKES A GREAT CANVAS.

NOW YOU'RE READY TO CUT. PROPER MEASUREMENT AND CUTTING IS CRITICAL. UNBALANCED KITES FLY IN CRAZY CIRCLES.

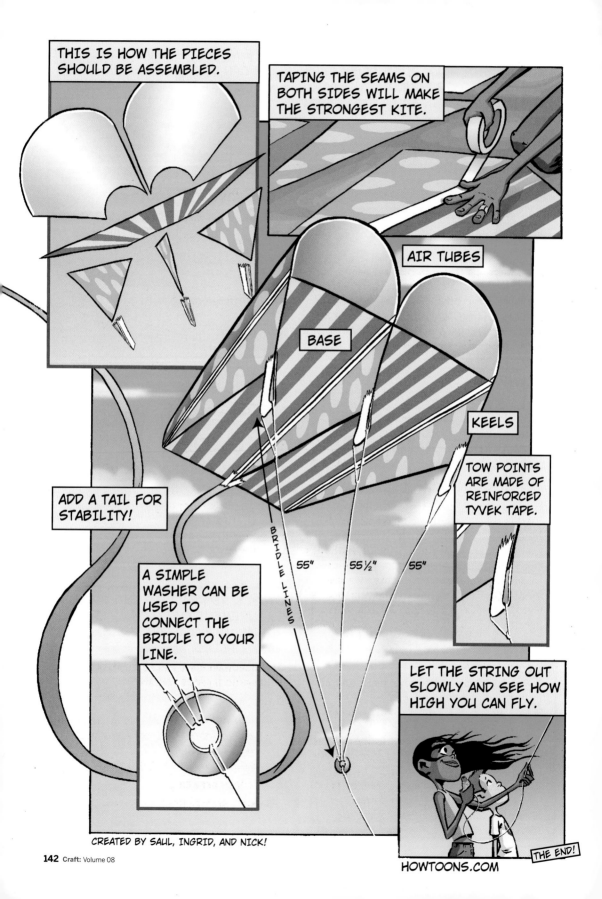

THIS IS HOW THE PIECES SHOULD BE ASSEMBLED.

TAPING THE SEAMS ON BOTH SIDES WILL MAKE THE STRONGEST KITE.

AIR TUBES

BASE

KEELS

ADD A TAIL FOR STABILITY!

TOW POINTS ARE MADE OF REINFORCED TYVEK TAPE.

A SIMPLE WASHER CAN BE USED TO CONNECT THE BRIDLE TO YOUR LINE.

BRIDLE LINES

55"   55½"   55"

LET THE STRING OUT SLOWLY AND SEE HOW HIGH YOU CAN FLY.

CREATED BY SAUL, INGRID, AND NICK!

THE END!

HOWTOONS.COM

Cathy Callahan
Old School

» Cathy Callahan is a crafter and window dresser who draws inspiration from vintage crafts. She blogs about 60s and 70s crafts at cathyofcalifornia.typepad.com.

Forever Flowers Fast

Dry your favorite varieties in the microwave in minutes!

Flowers and flower forms have been a big theme in crafts for decades. In the 1960s and 70s, flowers made with tissue paper, feathers, foil, macaroni, or paper cups were all the rage. I remember my mother making lupines by looping plastic six-pack holders around wire, then spray-painting them purple. They made a lovely centerpiece at the PTA luncheon.

But how about using the actual flowers? The art of drying and preserving flowers has been traced back to prehistoric times. It just might be the original craft.

We've all taken a special flower and pressed it between the pages of a book, like I did with my prom corsage. Had I known that there's more to it, I wouldn't have ended up with the moldy mess that I did. Since the beauty of fresh flowers only lasts a few days, you have to take steps to preserve them.

I really wanted to do it right this time, so I did a little research. It turns out that pressing takes about 2 weeks and drying can take up to 7 days. Who has time for that?

I almost gave up until I ran across an article entitled "Dry Flowers in Your Microwave in Minutes!" from *Drying Flowers with Silica Gel* (Hazel Pearson Handicrafts, 1975). Now there's no stopping me.

QUICK-DRIED FLOWERS

1. Cut the stem to 1".
2. Pour 1½" of silica gel to cover the bottom of the pan.
3. Place the flower face up and cover it completely with silica gel.
4. Put the pan in the microwave along with a glass of water (following all safety precautions for your microwave).
5. Zap. I zapped my daisies for 2 minutes, at 1-minute increments on medium power.
6. Take the pan out and allow it to cool for 15–20 minutes.

7. Gently remove the flower using a skewer, and shake off the silica gel.
8. Remove any excess silica gel with a soft brush.
9. Display as you like. I decorated a frame with some vintage trim as a showcase for my flowers.

MATERIALS

- » **MICROWAVE-SAFE PAN** I USED AN OLD PLASTIC TAKEOUT CONTAINER.
- » **FLOWERS**
- » **SILICA GEL** FROM THE FLORAL SECTION AT THE CRAFT STORE. THE PACKAGE SHOULD HAVE DIRECTIONS AND DRYING TIMES FOR DIFFERENT VARIETIES OF FLOWERS.
- » **WOODEN SKEWER**
- » **SMALL SOFT PAINTBRUSH**

Photograph by Cathy Callahan

BAZAAR

CRAFTY GOODS WE ADORE. *Compiled by Natalie Zee Drieu*

Egg Press Stitch Kits

$26
eggpress.com

Egg Press, known for beautiful letterpress cards, has moved into the world of DIY with the Egg Press Stitch Kits. The DIY pillow kits feature such cute illustrated characters as Magnus the monkey, Clauss the raccoon, and Perry the snail. Each hand-silk-screened canvas comes printed with outlines for precise clipping and stitch lines for sewing. The cuddly pillows are easy enough to sew by hand or by machine.

—*Natalie Zee Drieu*

Moxie's Flower Flair Pin Needle Felting Kit

$16
madebymoxie.etsy.com

A year ago, Moxie taught me how to needle-felt wool fiber, and I became addicted. She was also a huge hit with curious crafters at Maker Faire — she's the ultimate needle felting teacher. The next best thing to attending one of her events is to snatch up one of her kits, like this one, to make flower flair pins. Plus, Moxie's kits use vegetable-based Green Cell Foam for felting (most use polyurethane foam, a non-biodegradable petroleum by-product). —NZD

➕ **Check out more of Moxie's kits at our own makershed.com.**

The Soapmaking Kit

By Victoria Pilar Horner $25

chroniclebooks.com

For years I loved making little handmade soaps for friends as gifts. *The Soapmaking Kit* makes it easy with this complete set that includes two reusable soap molds, soap coloring, an illustrated booklet on how to get started, and dreamy lavender oil to scent your soaps. It's a great quick craft and perfect when you need to make gifts. —NZD

Knitter's Block

$48
cocoknits.com

I never used to block my knitting projects, but finally tried it after some baby booties came off the needles looking pretty twisted. Blocking those was a breeze, but then my outlook soured when I tried to put the finishing touches on a blanket. Enter Knitter's Block! This kit is a great resource — the modular, textured tiles fit together for different-shaped projects and come with a little vial of straight pins and a cotton cover for steam or dry blocking. There's also a handy booklet that clarifies the techniques and advises which method to use for which yarns. Rejoice!
—*Arwen O'Reilly Griffith*

Crybaby's Boutique »

crybabysboutique.com

The online fabric store Crybaby's Boutique features fabrics of all sorts, but believe me you'll swoon over the jersey knits. This season it's all about the jersey! The site has the widest array of jersey and knit fabrics I've ever seen, showcasing print after print of flowers, stars, stripes, polka dots, and more. First-time customers can sign up for a new account and receive 10% off their first order right away. —NZD

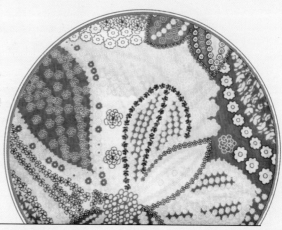

Aleene's Craft Glues

$2–$6

michaels.com

No matter what you're crafting, Aleene's Original Tacky Glue is fantastic to work with: it joins beautifully, dries clear, and is nontoxic. I love using it for craft projects and jewelry, or for mending things quickly.

  This legendary glue was invented more than 50 years ago by craft queen Aleene Jackson, and today there are newer spinoffs: Jewelry & Metal Glue for embellishing with metal, glass, or plastic, or Fabric Fusion for washable fabric crafts.
—Susan Beal

Tender Buttons

143 East 62nd Street, New York City

Walking into this tiny store is literally like entering another world, a world in which buttons are language, art, and commerce all rolled into one. Floor-to-ceiling shelves house hundreds of boxes of new, antique, and artisan-crafted buttons, from handmade Czech glass baubles, to vintage leather toggles, to plain but perfect four-holes.

  This is definitely the place to come if you're looking to match a missing button, but you may be seduced into buying something totally different, slightly impractical, and utterly delicious. The owners know everything there is to know about buttons, and a wall display of beautiful framed buttons from different eras makes this not just a store, but a destination. —AG

CRAFT LOOKS AT BOOKS

« Amy Butler's Little Stitches for Little Ones

By Amy Butler Chronicle Books $25

chroniclebooks.com

With my own baby on the way this fall, I was excited to see Amy Butler's new book of stylish sewing patterns for babies and kids. With so much to choose from, including clothing, nursery décor, and toys, I can make stylish baby gear of my own. The spiral-bound book contains beautiful photos and a front pocket full of sewing patterns for 20 projects. It's also filled with great tips, such as how to choose baby-friendly fabrics. —NZD

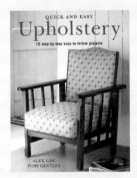

« Quick and Easy Upholstery

By Alex Law and Posy Gentles Cico Books $25

amazon.com

After I took an upholstery class last year, I was disappointed that I couldn't find a good reference book. *Quick and Easy Upholstery* does a pretty darn good job of filling the gap! Not only are the instructions clear and well-photographed, I also like the aesthetic of the makeovers done throughout the book. This is the perfect resource if you want to explore upholstery beyond the "101: Upholstery" article in *CRAFT, Volume 07.* —AG

« Lotta Prints

By Lotta Jansdotter Chronicle Books $20

chroniclebooks.com

My heart skipped a beat when I laid my hands on this enticing little book. I've long been a fan of Lotta Jansdotter's wonderful prints and have secretly been yearning to try printing myself — someday, when I had enough time. The book covers everything from rubber and potato stamps to linoleum block printing, expanding my preconceptions of what would be good materials or subjects. Jansdotter also includes photos of her own sketchbooks and things that inspire her, so you get a glimpse of her design process. —AG

« The Art of Felt

By Françoise Tellier-Loumagne Thames & Hudson $40

amazon.com

The Art of Felt is a stunning book on the subject of felt making. Tellier-Loumagne has created countless varieties of felt and she shows them alongside the images from nature that inspired them. The book is not project-based, but there are some simple tutorials for the curious. Whether it's wet felt, needle felt, or industrial waste fiber, this book shows how to use fiber to evoke the sky, clouds, sun, moon, stars, storms, and sunsets. —Brookelynn Morris

Susan Brackney
Recycle It

» An all-around bottle cap appreciator, Susan Brackney is an avid crafter, beekeeper, and the author of *The Lost Soul Companion: Comfort and Constructive Advice for Black Sheep, Square Pegs, Struggling Artists, and Other Free Spirits.*

Bottle Cap Madness

Make magnets, jewelry, and more with these underappreciated nuggets.

Somewhere in the world, there are drunken revelers crooning about 100 bottles of beer on the wall. Meanwhile, I fret about the scores of precious bottle caps that will go to waste. The Red Stripes. The Heinekens. The occasional Labatt. They're all so varied and colorful — not to mention sturdy enough to be the stuff of real crafting.

Relatively unadulterated, individual bottle caps become miniature, scallop-edged frames. And a bottle cap's exterior has its own allure. Caps with interesting typography, the odd anchor or crown, or, say, highly stylized birds, dragons, or other creatures are particularly beguiling.

Best of all, bottle caps are often free for the taking, they're easy to collect and store, and you don't need fancy tools to work with them. A hammer, a nail punch, and some wire, perhaps, or strong glue, resin, and a magnet or two are all you need to get started.

AMASSING YOUR STASH

You shouldn't have to drink yourself into a stupor to get loads of good bottle caps. If you ask nicely, restaurants and bars are usually happy to part with them. Just be sure to rinse them well and allow them to dry completely.

If it's vintage bottle caps you're after, things get a little trickier. Valuable both to collectors and to crafters, vintage caps can be costly and scarce. Laura and Benjamin Beamer, of Oakridge, Ore., have created high-end jewelry with vintage caps since 2000. The couple has collected nearly 4,000 unique bottle caps and well over 100,000 in all, which they've meticulously sorted by kind and condition and placed in hardware store-type drawers.

Set aside your favorite bottle cap designs, and sort the rest by color, so you'll be ready when inspiration hits.

BOTTLE CAP MAGNET: USING BOTTLE CAPS "AS IS"

1. Copy or draw an image onto heavy paper or cardstock, then carefully cut out a small circle with the image in its center.

2. Glue the image into the inside of your bottle cap.

3. After the glue has dried, paint on clear nail polish or mix a small amount of clear resin and pour it onto the image seated inside the bottle cap. Kerry Casey of Cornwall, N.Y., sells her wares on Etsy and says that when it comes to pouring resin, less is more. "I've found that if you're looking for a crisp, clean image, less resin is better."

4. You may notice some bubbles forming as you pour the resin into your cap. To de-gas a resin product such as Envirotex Lite, lightly blow on its surface, or save your breath and use a hair dryer. "When I'm doing a whole bunch of [magnets] at a time, I get the bubbles out with a blowtorch," Casey says.

5. Once the interior of your bottle cap has dried and cured, you can glue a small magnet to its exterior, allow it to dry completely, and voilà!

PENDANTS AND PURSES: THE HOLE STORY

1. To make a simple pendant, use a 1/16" metal punch to make a small hole along the top edge of your bottle cap.

2. Follow the Bottle Cap Magnet steps 1–4, taking care not to cover the hole you just made with resin.

Photography by Beamer Arts Desigh (above and B); Kerry Casey (A); Susan Brackney (C); Beck Underwood (D)

Fig. A: Bottle cap magnets. Fig. B: This charm bracelet was worked with a jeweler's precision. Fig. C: Bottle caps make up the chains around this mirror frame. Fig. D: Another bottle cap chain comes to life.

3. Once the cap has dried and cured, insert a split ring into the hole, clamp shut with needlenose pliers, then run your desired length of ball chain through the split ring.

4. Willing to bore a few more holes per cap? Janet Cooper, of Sheffield, Mass., flattens vintage bottle caps in a large press and then joins them to one another in 4 spots to create a chain mail effect for her bottle cap purses.

ROPES AND SNAKES

For more than a decade, Beck Underwood of New York City has linked ordinary bottle caps to create sundry snakes and skeletons. Underwood punches a hole through the center of each cap with a large nail and hammer, 20 or 30 at a time.

1. To make a folk art-style snake that's 2' long, drill or punch a hole through the center of 120 bottle caps.

2. String the caps one by one, each facing the same direction, onto heavy-gauge steel wire (aluminum might break). Secure one end using the needlenose pliers, an eye hook or other fastener, and a large bead or block (the snake's tail).

3. Once all the caps have been strung, again use the needlenose pliers to close and attach the remaining bottle cap rope end to a piece of scrap wood. This will serve as your snake's head.

4. Embellish the wooden head and tail parts with acrylic paints, and seal with clear acrylic spray finish. If it's going outdoors, hit the bottle cap rope portion with the spray finish, too.

Grace Bonney
DIY Design

» Grace Bonney is a Brooklyn-based freelance writer and the founder/ editor of Design*Sponge (designspongeonline.com), a website devoted to design. She also runs a national series of Biz Lady Meetups, designed to connect women who run design-based businesses.

Lofty Inspiration

DIY puts a new spin on classic design.

As I opened my laptop and got ready to start the day, I caught the subject line of my first email: "George Nelson would totally hate you." Not words anyone wants to read when welcoming a new morning, but I can't say I didn't see it coming.

Recently, there's been a debate between DIYers and design enthusiasts over whether it's appropriate to create handmade versions of classic, high-end designs. As a design blogger I see projects like these every day, and over the past four years I've seen an exponential rise in their popularity.

While sifting through entries from a DIY contest I held on my blog, I came across a particularly interesting project from clothing designer Angie Johnson of Headquarters Galerie in Montreal. Inspired by George Nelson's classic Miniature Chests, Johnson decided to create her own version using a little elbow grease and inexpensive parts she found at Ikea. I admired Johnson's creativity and the level of personalization she'd achieved on a tight budget. George Nelson's original design runs around $1,400, while Johnson's project cost just over $100.

Despite some angry emails chiding me for posting the project, Johnson went on to win fourth place in the competition, supported by a large number of readers and DIY fans across the web.

Johnson's success represents a shift in the design world. For some time, crafters have eschewed pre-made, cookie-cutter products, but now seem to be rethinking these mass-market resources, modding them into creations of their own.

Sites like Ikea Hacker (a blog devoted to showcasing "hacked" or customized Ikea items) and the rising popularity of projects like Johnson's are further proof that DIYers are interested in putting their own stamp on the products they bring into their homes.

Whether you paint, upholster, or hack inexpensive materials into something special, this trend in DIY culture boils down to a desire to reflect personal values. For Johnson, it was important to support local, independent artists whenever possible.

"So many stores are carrying affordable, more professional, and cuter supplies these days," she says. "With options like that, I'd much rather build something on my own than splurge on something that isn't necessary. I loved George Nelson's Miniature Chest but [I'd rather] spend $1,400 supporting independent jewelry designers [whose work I would keep in the chest] than on the storage piece itself."

Whether the motivation is based on financial or ethical concerns, the message is clear: to create something with your own hands is about feeling a sense of accomplishment. Even if inspiration comes from a high-end design, the final result is a piece of furniture that reminds you of the hard work that you, the maker, put into the world.

MATERIALS

» **FIRA CHESTS FROM IKEA (3)**

» **FORNBRO SIDE TABLE FROM IKEA** AVAILABLE FROM CRAIGSLIST OR EBAY, OR ANOTHER SUITABLE SET OF TABLE LEGS.

» **FINE-GRIT SANDING SPONGE**

» **COTTON RAGS**

» **RUBBER GLOVES, DUST MASK**

» **STAIN** IN YOUR CHOICE OF COLOR

» **SPRAY VARNISH (6 CANS)**

» **WRAPPING PAPER OR WALLPAPER SCRAPS** FOR LINING

» **FELT**

» **WHITE CRAFT GLUE**

» **NO MORE NAILS OR SIMILAR ADHESIVE**

GEORGE NELSON-INSPIRED JEWELRY CHEST

1. Assemble the Fira chests.
Follow Ikea's written instructions.

2. Sand the chests.
Smooth off the edges with the sanding sponge. This is not the best quality wood, so these early prep stages are important to do properly. It can make the difference between a smooth finish and a dull, unprofessional look.

3. Stain the chests.
Add 2 coats of stain using a rag instead of a brush. Wipe on the varnish with one rag, then wipe off the excess with a clean rag. Keep a steady supply of rags handy, and wear rubber gloves to avoid staining your skin. Let the stain dry.

4. Sand again.
After staining, give the chests a light sanding, and wipe away dust with a large dry paintbrush or clean dry cloth.

5. Varnish the chests.
You can use a spray varnish to get a nice, even coat. Slow and steady wins the race with this task. You can add a plastic handle that attaches to the spray can, which makes spraying easier and gives your finger a break.

You'll need about 8 coats of varnish with some light sanding after the second and sixth coats. Make sure to varnish in a well-ventilated area, and wear a mask if possible.

6. Line the drawers.
After the varnish has dried completely (leave it overnight at least), line the inside of the drawers. Johnson used vintage wrapping paper. She measured and cut it to size, then glued it on with some watered-down white craft glue and an old paintbrush. She used the end of the paintbrush to smooth out the paper as she went. This method helps avoid bubbles and lumps.

Johnson also lined the bottom of the drawers with cream-colored felt. She didn't glue it down, in case she wanted to change the color. As long as it fits snugly, it isn't going anywhere.

Photography by Angie Johnson

A
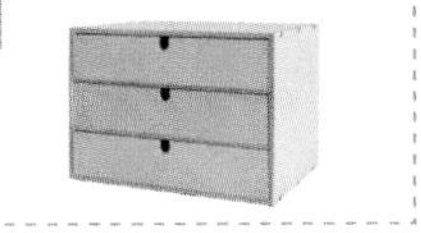

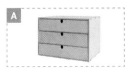

Figs. A & B: Ikea Fira chest or Nelson? Fig. C: Attach the table base. Figs. D & E: Jewel-perfect drawers.

B
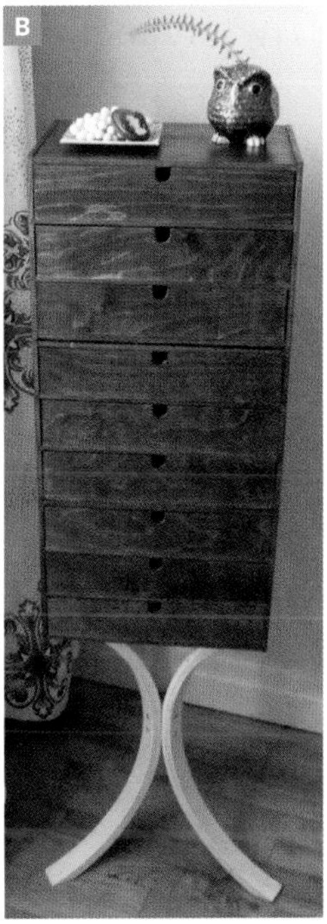

C
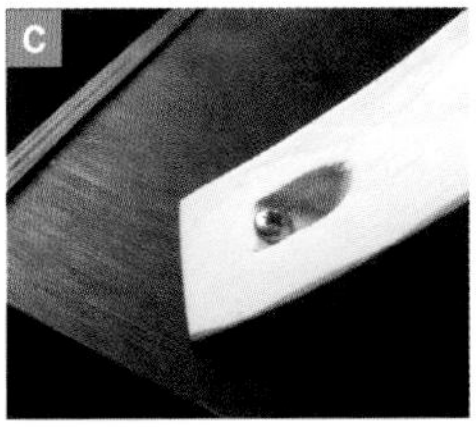

D
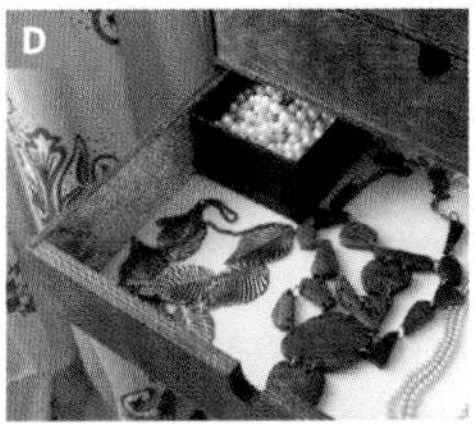

E
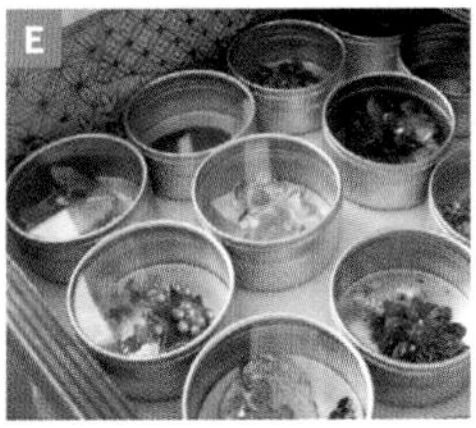

7. Attach the Fornbro table base.
Using small screws no deeper than the thickness of the wood, attach the table base to one of the chests. You can also use No More Nails glue for extra security (let it dry 24 hours). For added stability, attach the round Fornbro tabletop to the base, then attach the tabletop to the chest.

8. Attach the chests to each other.
Zigzag heavy-duty glue in the centers of the chest bottoms and tops that you want to stack, and tightly attach them to each other. No More Nails works great for this, but a lot of other types of thick glue could work, too.

TIP: **To keep all her earrings and necklaces untangled, Johnson used metal watchmaker's cases with glass lids from Lee Valley Tools. They come in many different sizes, are surprisingly affordable, and have the added benefit of allowing you to see your jewelry through the glass lids.** leevalley.com

Wendy Tremayne
Re: Fitted

» Wendy Tremayne (gaiatreehouse.com) is renovating an RV park into a 100% reuse, off-grid B&B in Truth or Consequences, N.M. Another project, Swap-O-Rama-Rama (swaporamarama.org), is a clothing swap and DIY workshop designed to offer people an alternative to consumerism.

Whimsies in Wool

Peggy Campbell's rugs give old sweaters a new purpose.

I once heard someone refer to a rug as a guest rather than a possession. A home without a carpet does feel lonely. We suspect that even our "guests" have a story to tell. We search them for traces of places, times, and people, for records of beliefs and events.

In Russian folk tales, the writings of Mark Twain, and the classic stories of *Arabian Nights*, the flying carpet traverses continents. Accompanied by the wind, it carries us through the colors of an ever-changing sky, animate, sturdy, luxurious, and able to deliver dreams.

Peggy Campbell is a modern rug maker. Her rag-rug creations are made from the once-loved sweaters of unknown others. Campbell wanted quality and found it in felted wool. She filled her loom with repurposed woven garments because they were available and they offered a great variety of color. Now she buys them in bulk from a textile supplier who provides reused materials.

From her father, who was a painter, Campbell inherited an appreciation for harmony in hue. Her rugs are a showcase for color. She sees a "blurred line" between art and what is utilitarian. "In the same way a painter puts paint on a canvas, I put colored warp and weft into my rugs," she says.

Campbell's home in Terrace Bay, Ontario, Canada, is adorned with her textured works in earthy colors. The lush, soft pieces make all who inhabit the space feel cozy.

Perhaps the magic carpet is hostage to the mythic realm, and not found in Campbell's living room, but pixie dust can be devised if one follows her mastered method. She invites us to materialize our own colorful world: a woolly nest for a cold room, a playful pad to welcome guests, a soft spot for a loved pet to doze upon, or a sphere of color simply to delight the imagination.

MATERIALS

» **2-HARNESS LOOM, 36" WIDE, ADAPTED TO WEAVE WITH RAGS** YOU CAN ALSO USE A SIMPLE FRAME LOOM; THERE'S ONE YOU CAN MAKE YOURSELF ON PAGE 58.

» **1-DENT REED** YOU'LL NEED TO MAKE THIS BY MODIFYING AN EXISTING REED TO MAKE IT 1 WIRE PER INCH.

» **SCISSORS**

» **MEASURING TAPE**

» **SEWING MACHINE**

» **WOOL SWEATERS (7–12)** TO MAKE 28 STRIPS OF RAG 6' LONG

FINISHED SIZE: 26"×46"

TERMS

Reed A comb, closed on both sides, that fits into the beater to beat the weft threads into place.

Dent A space in the reed. Reeds are measured in dents per inch.

Sley To thread the warp ends through the dents in the reed.

Heddle A device that raises and lowers the warp threads. It can be a rigid piece of wood, metal, or plastic, or a series of wire or cord loops connected to a shaft.

Shed The space that forms when the warp is raised to allow a shuttle to pass through.

Selvedges Edges of the web of cloth being woven.

WOVEN RUG FROM SWEATERS

1. Full the sweaters.
Wash the wool sweaters in hot and then cold water until they're felted, so they don't unravel when cut.

2. Cut the sweaters into strips.
Once dry, cut sweaters into 1¼"–1½" rag strips, starting at the bottom of the sweater. Cut 1 continuous strip (Figures A and B).

3. Warp the loom.
Allow for fringe and loom waste: warp 1epi (ends per inch), 28" wide, 28 warp ends, 2yds long (Figure C).

4. Sley 1 warp end per dent.
Center your warp on the loom and tie each warp thread (rag) onto the back or top beam using a half hitch knot (Figure D). The warp is the length of your rug.

5. Thread the rags.
Thread the rags through the heddles and your reed (Figure E). Wind the warp onto the back beam. Tie the warp onto your front apron (front beam) using a reef knot. Check for even tension (Figure F).

6. Lay the weft loosely in the shed.
Allow about 8"–10" including tie-on for fringe. Leave an 8" tail and weave it back in on itself (Figure G). Beat firmly.

7. Weave, sewing the rag ends together.
Join ends with a sewing machine when you change color (Figure H). Weave the rug (Figure I) until you can no longer advance the warp. Watch your selvedges and measure to see that they remain even.

8. Untie the warp and knot the fringe.
Untie 2 warp threads at a time from the top of the loom (Figure J). Tie these threads in a reef knot close to the rug to make your fringe (Figure K). Continue tying, 2 by 2, until you have the top edge finished. Repeat on the bottom (Figure L).

9. Trim the ends.
Lay the rug out on the floor and trim the fringe to your desired length.

➕ You can see more of Peggy Campbell's work at fiveforty.etsy.com and icraft.ca/five_forty.

Etsy

FeltInspired
Accessories $42

crescentwench
Clothing $45

JessicaDoyle
Art $10

NightByrd
Housewares $225

polarity
Jewelry $18

ThePettisCollection
Accessories $10

jilldrapermakes-
stuff $26

jorgensenstudio
Jewelry $37

happywhosits
Patterns $5

underthewire
Jewelry $54

pdxbeanies
Children $24

bigpinkheart
Bags & Purses $18

siouxsane
Art $85

wigglytoothfactory
Children $20

NestaHome
Housewares $55

MetalheartDesign
Jewelry $32

BeadersBoutique
Supplies $11

matsudabunch
Jewelry $23

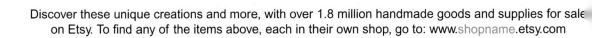

Discover these unique creations and more, with over 1.8 million handmade goods and supplies for sale on Etsy. To find any of the items above, each in their own shop, go to: www.shopname.etsy.com

sticknymph
Paper Goods — $10

bluevalentinepress
Books & Zines — $26

kimquinndotcom
Jewelry — $27

reiter8
Bags & Purses — $125

ThePlayfulNeedle
Children — $24

happyowl
Glass — $25

auntiejill
Children — $35

SimplyWired
Jewelry — $38

GretchenKramp
Ceramics — $14

theRockInspired
Jewelry — $45

merkabajewelry
Jewelry — $18

samisue
Clothing — $58

sproutonline
Jewelry — $45

triflydesign
Housewares — $35

flurrsprite
Books & Zines — $35

fabricfarrago
Jewelry — $22

underroos
Toys — $15

tomokotahara
Accessories — $45

Buy Handmade

▶◀ Though she's consumed with studying 19th-century British novels for her dissertation, Columbia University grad student **Anna Wulick** still manages to look to the next century: the designers of the 1950s.

During a recent apartment "update," she noticed the faux velvet riding toy someone had given her 2-year-old daughter. She ripped off the purple snail top to discover an elegant, minimalist rocker underneath. A hands-on crafter since high school, Wulick "will launch in to do almost anything for which I can reasonably approximate the necessary equipment."

Using a heavy canvas from the As-Is bin at Ikea, she deftly reworked the gaudy toddler toy into a streamlined ride. "I hadn't done upholstery before," she says, "but I figured it was reasonably intuitive — you know, sew fabric around this object." Not that Wulick's new field of toy upholstery was an easy one. "This rocker is designed fairly poorly, so in order to upholster it, I basically had to sew the fabric right onto it by hand." The end result would look right at home in Alvar Aalto's nursery.

So how does someone who relishes working with her hands balance that with hours staring at the page? Crafting and writing "are actually quite a nice refuge from each other," Wulick admits. The "delayed gratification" of spending years on a dissertation contrasts with the "almost instant results" of crafting, whether it's making paintings for her Etsy shop, Forty-Two Roads, or reupholstering office chairs for her home. Plus, "both do require a lot of attention to detail and the ability to plan ahead, so I guess some of the skills overlap," Wulick notes.

And there may be something in the self-reliant cultural attitudes of Wulick's 19th-century subjects that inspires her handiwork. "Whenever I think of something I want, I tend to just assume that I can make it myself rather than buy it. I love working with my hands so much that the process itself is probably my favorite part of any project."

—Arwen O'Reilly Griffith

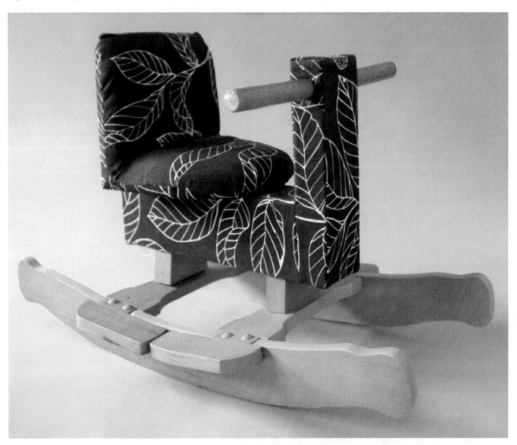

Photograph by Dustin Fenstermacher